The Golden Compass
and Philosophy

Popular Culture and Philosophy®
Series Editor: George A. Reisch

For full details of all Popular Culture and Philosophy® books, visit www.opencourtbooks.com.

Popular Culture and Philosophy®

The Golden Compass and Philosophy

God Bites the Dust

Edited by
RICHARD GREENE
and
RACHEL ROBISON

OPEN COURT
Chicago and La Salle, Illinois

Volume 43 in the series, Popular Culture and Philosophy™,
edited by George A. Reisch

**To order books from Open Court, call toll-free 1-800-815-2280,
or visit our website at www.opencourtbooks.com.**

Open Court Publishing Company is a division of Carus Publishing
Company.

Library of Congress Cataloging-in-Publication Data

The golden compass and philosophy : God bites the dust / edited by
Richard Greene and Rachel Robison..
     p. cm. —(Popular culture and philosophy ; v. 43)
    Includes bibliographical references and index.
    ISBN-13: 978-0-8126-9671-4 (trade paper : alk. paper)
    1. Pullman, Philip, 1946- Northern lights. 2. Pullman, Philip,
1946—Philosophy. 3. Children's stories, English—History and
criticism. 4 Fantasy fiction, English—History and criticism.
5. Philosophy in literature.
    I. Greene, Richard, 1961 Sept. 2- II. Robison, Rachel, 1983-
    PR6066.U44Z665 2009
    823'.914—dc22

                       2009030679

For Sharon, Neal, Susan, Cheryl, Kris, Jason, Brooke, Becca, Clint, and Henry

Contents

Part I
When You Stopped Believing in God Did You Stop Believing in Good and Evil?

Part II
Tell Them Stories. They Need the Truth. You Must Tell Them True Stories, and Everything Will Be Well, Just Tell Them Stories.

Acknowledgments

Working on this project has been a pleasure, in no small part because of the many fine folks who have assisted us along the way. In particular a debt of gratitude is owed to George Reisch and David Ramsay Steele at Open Court, the contributors to this volume, and our respective academic departments at UMass Amherst and Weber State University. We would also like to express a warm thanks to Angie Harris and Pat Pinsent who each recommended other contributors to this collection. Finally, we'd like to thank those family members, students, friends, and colleagues (and their dæmons) with whom we've had fruitful and rewarding conversations on various aspects of all things *His Dark Materials* as it relates to philosophical themes.

Angels and Dæmons and Bears (Oh My)!

Since Pullman's *His Dark Materials* trilogy is ostensibly to some degree about Catholicism, we thought it would be appropriate to start this book with a confession.

When *His Dark Materials* was recommended to one of us (we won't say which one) some years back as a philosophically compelling read, he thought to himself, "But isn't that a children's book series? . . . How could it possibly be philosophically sophisticated while targeting an adolescent audience?"

But as soon as he started on *The Golden Compass*, he discovered how wrong he'd been. It was noticeable from the first few pages that the universe Pullman had created for his readers was not merely the setting for a gripping fantasy adventure, but also a world with a rich metaphysics. Not many pages later, it became clear that the work also posed fascinating epistemic questions, intriguing ethical dilemmas, and imaginative fictional responses to age-old philosophical issues.

In short, *His Dark Materials* is not just for kids, and is rich in philosophical delights.

Passionate controversy has attended Pullman's trilogy since its publication, rising to a climax with the release of the *Golden Compass* movie. In light of the attitude that Pullman takes in the novels (and in a number of interviews) toward God and organized religion, many religious people felt that the subject matter was not appropriate for its intended audience. This controversy presented another set of philosophical issues to be grappled with in this volume. Is exposing children to views that are critical of religious institutions and belief in God tantamount to committing an act of spiritual violence, or does such exposure to critical assessment of accepted social practices teach children to think carefully about the things they are taught rather than blindly following authority? Does exposing children to the idea that God may himself be feeble and corrupt threaten to leave young readers jaded, or does it suggest to them the possibility that they might, like Lyra, embrace their own life as their own without viewing their very nature as inherently sinful?

Pullman offers Lyra as a model of the attitude that one should take toward living their life, but he also has quite a bit to say about what happens after we die. The afterlife in Pullman's universe is far from the final and eternal reward that Christianity promises. The dead do not exist in a paradise rich with positive experiences, but they are not in hell either. They are left in a drab place for eternity to reflect on their lives. Lyra comes to free them and they are given a choice to remain in the world of the dead or join the universe in the form of Dust. Why would anyone make this choice? The answer lies within these pages.

The world of the dead is not the only world we are introduced to in *His Dark Materials*. We meet characters from our own world, from worlds close to ours, from distant worlds, and from the worlds of the Gods. Inhabiting these worlds are a variety of creatures such as witches, armored bears, wheeled creatures called mulefa, Gallevespians, angels, harpies, specters, and most importantly humans and their dæmons. Dæmons present a number of puzzling philosophical problems for personal identity and soul-body interaction.

It will be our pleasure (along with our authors) to guide you through these worlds and introduce you these wonderful and philosophically interesting characters. So wield your subtle knife, consult your golden compass, and gaze through you amber spyglass as we follow Lyra on her journey. Our sincere hope is that we can do the same degree of justice to Pullman's work that he did to Milton and Nietzsche (he made Milton fun and made Nietzsche appear sane).

PART I

When You Stopped Believing in God Did You Stop Believing in Good and Evil?

1

Thus Spake Philip Pullman

RANDALL E. AUXIER

Mrs. Coulter: The Overwoman?

She's Cleopatra and Mata Hari and Madame Bovary and Joan of Arc all rolled into one, isn't she? Maybe you should add in your favorite Bond Girl to complete the list. And I don't know about you, but I don't really picture Nicole Kidman when I try to imagine her. Don't get me wrong, I'm a huge fan of Nicole Kidman, but she just doesn't quite have the right *femme fatale* sort of energy (plenty *femme*, not enough *fatale*). And Mrs. Coulter is so far beyond *Noir*, anyway, don't you think? So I can't quite imagine, well, *whom* to imagine when I try to bring her to my mind's eye.

But I am going to have to confess something. I don't really dislike Mrs. Coulter as much I'm supposed to. In fact, I have a silly crush on her more wicked side. Part of it is that I can't quite get her character to "hang together" in my mind, which is intriguing all by itself. She's a deliciously mysterious babe, and quite a dangerous one to have around (ask Lord Boreal). And part of the attraction is that she's a fictional character, which is the safest sort of dangerous woman to be infatuated with.

So there you have it: she's dangerous *and* she's safely non-existent, and I think about her all the time (well a lot of the time). It could be a problem. But only because I *always* think too much about nothing very important. Fortunately, that's my job. Good work if you can get it (and keep it).

My Theory

So I came up with a theory. Philosophers like theories quite a lot. Not so much as we like chocolatl, but chocolatl doesn't pay our bills and theories do (oddly enough). I started off just wondering whether Mrs. Coulter is really religious at all (it would spoil the attraction if she were, don't ask me why). Her ambiguous religiosity seemed to be at the heart of the puzzle, or so I hypothesized, and since it was *my* puzzle, no one prevented me from thinking so.

It's not easy to tell the difference, by the bye, between good philosophy and people just thinking stuff up. If you're beginning to get the sense that philosophers sit around making stuff up, I would say you're getting the message here. I'm going to do what I can in these pages to show you a few things about how to make stuff up and call it philosophy (and get away with it). Sociologists and psychologists also make things up, but (from what I can tell) their theories need not have anything to do with reality, so philosophy is more constrained.

Back to my theory. I decided that there are two main ways we might understand Mrs. Coulter's obsessions and motives (this is how philosophical theories usually start: on the one hand . . . on the other hand . . .). First, Philip Pullman offers, on several occasions, the suggestion that Mrs. Coulter is *afraid* of Dust and genuinely wants to use the power of "experimental theology" to spare people from sin in the future. You gotta love the idea that what we call "physics" could have been "experimental theology" had a few things been different in our world (like the hilariously creative notion that John Calvin becomes Pope).

Anyway, we might call this anti-Dust crusader the "religious" version of the Coulter character. But on many other occasions, Pullman suggests that Mrs. Coulter is really only interested in power, and she uses all the means available to a woman in her world to gain it. In her quest for power, she doesn't seem to be afraid of *anything*, least of all sin. On the face of it, these seem like two different people. I will get to the bottom of this with my theory, and I hope to get it done before Mrs. Coulter gets to the bottom of the Abyss.

I think that there's a sort of genius in the way Pullman finishes off Mrs. Coulter: locked in an eternal struggle with Metatron, who symbolizes the *religious* craving for power, in all its perversity, and Lord Asriel, who symbolizes its contrary, the *worldly* will to power, all falling forever together, kicking, biting, pulling hair. Their plunge is, I think, intended to allude to the fall of the angels banished from heaven in Milton's *Paradise Lost* (I, 44–75; VI, 860–877). But what would you bet that Mrs. Coulter switches sides whenever either Metatron or Asriel gets the upper hand in that endless struggle? And they all fall into a pit so deep that a physical body would starve before it hits the bottom (to use Pullman's image), and then their ghosts continue falling and fighting forevermore. I think that Pullman was telling us not to expect a final resolution between these contending forces, but Mrs. Coulter seems to hold them in balance by never quite committing herself wholly to one or the other.

There is a good deal to think about here. I had so many questions and so few answers. So I did what anyone with too much free time would have done: I started poking around in likely books to see where Pullman got all this stuff, and to try to figure out his angle on Mrs. Coulter. I went looking specifically for a model for her character in all this ancient sacred literature and also in John Milton, who were sources for this story. I think I found Mrs. Coulter, but I will save that for near the end (don't peek).

Paradise Re-lost

Lots of people have commented that Pullman sort of rewrote Milton's big ol' poem about the war in heaven and turned the story on its head. In terms of the *content* of the trilogy, I think there is a pretty good case for seeing it this way. But what is going on *philosophically* with Pullman is really a different story.

Let's cover Milton first. You may recall that in the days before the world was created, a third of the angels took up battle with the Almighty. It didn't turn out well for anybody, really. Maybe Pullman didn't buy the way Milton depicted Adam's attitude toward the tragedy of world history near the end of the big ol' poem, when our common progenitor pretended to be grateful for all the blood, sweat and tears shed by his many sons and daughters, just so that his heirs could be "saved" later on. Well, did Pullman rewrite Milton? Was that what he set out to do?

Someone had to "take one for the team," so I did it. I went and reread *Paradise Lost* to see what all came from there that later shows up in Pullman's trilogy. I found some stuff that others haven't noticed, mainly because no one really wanted to reread the whole thing. Do they still teach Milton in high school? God, when I was a youngster, everyone had to read this blasted thing, which

I always wanted to rename "Boredom Gained." But I now know that it's a better read when you get older.[1] Anyway, here is some stuff I found.

Many Worlds

One doesn't need recent physicists like Hugh Everett (1930–1982) to find the "many worlds" hypothesis, although Pullman does have Mary Malone mention Everett's hypothesis by name in Book III (AS, p. 77). Milton already had a similar idea: "Space may produce new worlds; whereof so rife / There went a fame in heav'n that He ere long intended to create" (I, 650–51). So there are many worlds. Further, the same idea occurs in the very line that gave our trilogy its name, where Milton says that all the several causes of the world would struggle in endless chaos, "Unless th' Almighty Maker them ordain / His dark materials to create more worlds" (II, 915–16). In fact, it is mildly un-Biblical (as Milton knew) to pretend that God made only one world. Certain passages, especially in Genesis, but also elsewhere, whenever angels are being discussed (such as Psalm 82, or Revelation), only make sense by supposing a vast cosmos of many worlds, and many levels of existence beyond our familiar realm of the senses.

The idea that these many worlds might exist right on top of each other in dimensions of possibility is not in Milton, however. So the business in Lyra's world about the "heretical" Barnard-Stokes Hypothesis (which is supposed to correspond to the Everett hypothesis) is only intended to remind us of how the Church has been suspicious, historically, of new ideas and science. This many worlds idea is not heretical in our world, so making it a part of a heresy in Lyra's world is a difference between hers and ours. I can't see that Milton would have had a problem with the plurality of worlds in dimensions of possibility. And the idea is probably not heretical.

---

[1] Okay, I'm not quite being truthful. I bought the audio book version and listened to it on a car trip to Kansas City. But I did dig out my old high school text book version, snickered at my comments in the margins from when I was seventeen, and marked it up anew as I came to things I recognized from Pullman. And I'm coming clean about this because I need you to be aware that there is a fantastic audio version of this book, read by Anton Lesser, whose vocal interpretation of the poem is so good that the whole thing became comprehensible to me for the first time. It's published by Naxos audio books and it is worth every cent of the $40.00 it costs.

Milton was very, very smart, and he was more than a poet. He wrote some philosophical prose that philosophers still read and teach, especially his defense of the free press. In the big ol' poem, he articulated a fairly subtle theory of knowledge, suggesting a dynamic physical intercourse (Milton loved the word "intercourse") between the worlds of spirit and sense. For example, the inhabitants of these two worlds might eat the same food (V, 475–505), which is probably why the angel Balthamos eats a mint cake when Will offers him one in Book III. But most importantly, the inhabitants of heavenly domains can have sex and reproduce with humans.

We will get to this point in a while, but I want to make it clear that Milton vehemently denied that it was sex between Adam and Eve that made them "fall." Milton explicitly has Adam and Eve doing the deed in paradise, and he says they would have had children, eventually. The difference is that there was no lust in the pre-fall intercourse of Adam and Eve. There was pleasure, but no lust, which I find a bit difficult to imagine, fallen sinner that I am. In any case, those who want to attack Pullman for promoting sex as a perfectly sinless thing should examine and compare his presentation of sex between Will and Lyra with Milton's description of sex between Adam and Eve *before* the Fall. My point for now is that angels are *physical* beings. The relevance of sex will become clearer in a few moments.

Dust to Dust

The idea of "Dust" is also in Milton, just before the line about "his dark materials." He's speaking of the elements and forces that make up the physical world, and he says that Hot, Cold, Moist, and Dry each have an army of particles contending with one another "unnumbered as the sands" and these atoms are "levied to side with warring winds," and "To whom these [particles] most adhere, / He rules a moment" (see II, 898–908). That explains a few things, like the dust winds discovered by Mary Malone on her platform high in the crown of the seed-pod trees. It also explains the relationship between Dust and the will to power. Such individuals as Mrs. Coulter and Lord Asriel are probably very dusty, but maybe not in quite the same way—for example, I think Asriel is probably Hot and Mrs. Coulter is probably Cold (that's my suggestion about why Pullman names her "Coulter" and insists on calling her that throughout the trilogy—she's a cold customer).

The idea of Dust occurs in much the same way that Pullman speaks of it near the end of Book I (GC, pp. 370–74, 376–77), when Lord Asriel is explaining to Lyra, in his comfy prison near Svalbard, where Dust comes from. Asriel quotes the famous Biblical passage from Genesis "for dust thou art and unto to dust shalt thou return" (GC, p. 373). Milton has Adam pondering this same admonition and his own "death," and Milton comments about whether our human inability to be satisfied might continue beyond death, but "That were to extend / His sentence beyond dust and Nature's law" (X, 805–06). In short, Milton is saying that desire and dissatisfaction die with physical death and do not extend beyond our dissolution to dust. Dust is an ultimate destiny for us, which is a point Pullman uses freely. It is not heresy unless Milton is a heretic (although plenty of people, such as William Blake, have said he was).

Also, the tradition of orthodox Christian theology makes a place for this sort of idea, this dissolution to dust. For example, when Macrina (324–379 c.e.) explained her theology to her brother, whom we now know as St. Gregory of Nyssa, he asked her how the final resurrection of the body is possible, given that the bodies of the disciples have (by the fourth century) dissolved into atoms. Macrina said that the atoms have known each other in life and will recognize one another when God ordains their rejoining. This is not heresy, it's integral to the Christian tradition, and it also turns out to be the truth about the physical universe. We now call it "quantum entanglement" (see AS, p. 156), and many of us don't expect God ever to ordain or command a final resurrection, but both Milton and Pullman are well aware that Christianity requires an interpretation of the simplest particles that compose the physical world. Pullman is not making this up and it isn't an inversion of Christian doctrine, or of Milton.

Touched by an Angel

Pullman's description of the huge battle between the forces of Lord Asriel and Metatron in Book III owes a good deal to Milton's description of the first war in heaven, a war replayed on the Plain of Armageddon in the Christian book of Revelation. Regarding this battle, Pullman suffers from the same sort of problem as Milton and the writer of Revelation: how does one describe in physical terms a conflict among angels, none of whom can quite be killed or even go to war in the ordinary sense? (see *Paradise Lost*, VI, 345–54) The writer of Revelation gets all symbolic and cryptic and indecipherable. Milton just has Raphael (the archangel who brings all the messages from God to Adam) lament that this is a "Sad task and hard, for how shall I relate / To human sense th' invisible exploits / Of warring spirits?" (V, 564–66) It just sounds silly when we bring it down to a level of description we can grasp. So the Archangel decides to describe it *as if* it were a war among human-like beings, and warns us that this is only an analogy.

This strategy is reminiscent of the disclaimer made by the first angels we meet in Pullman's Book II, when Queen Ruta Skadi encounters angels who look like human forms to her only because she is unaware "that she saw them as human-formed only because she expected to" and that really they were more "like architecture than organism, huge structures composed of intelligence and feeling" (SK, p. 141). This corresponds to Milton's description of angelic nature as "All heart they live, all head, all eye, all ear / All intellect, all sense; and as they please / They limb themselves, and color, shape, or size / Assume, as likes them best, condense or rare" (VI, 350–54). This explains why Balthamos can play the part of Will's dæmon if he so chooses, and why it is humiliating for him to condense himself in a mere bird. Much of Pullman's angelology follows Milton, but both also follow certain older texts. St. Augustine's views are explicitly mentioned, but also there are the shared sources of the Bible and the *Pseudepigrapha*. I'll get to that in a minute, since I know you're just dying to find out all this stuff.

But the idea that humans of flesh and blood can sometimes become angels is also in Milton, in much the way Pullman describes it. Remember that Balthamos was *always* an angel, but he helped Baruch, who had been a man, the brother of Enoch, *become* an angel; meanwhile, the Authority also made Enoch an angel, renamed "Metatron." Milton says that men and angels differ in degree but are of the same kind (V, 490), and has Raphael say to Adam: "Wonder not then, what God for you saw good / If I refuse not, but convert, as you, / To proper substance. Time may come when men / With angels may participate, and find / No inconvenient diet, nor too light fare; / Your bodies may at last turn all to spirit, / Improved by tract of time, and winged ascend / Ethereal as we, or may, at choice / Here or in heav'nly paradises dwell" (V, 491–501). So, it looks to me like Pullman intends to stick with Milton on this relationship between angels and humans, and if you found Pullman's description of angels a bit unfamiliar, it's because you forgot how it works in *Paradise Lost* (or because you never read that far).

That Knife

The subtle knife itself also comes from Milton, at least partly. It's modeled on the sword of Michael, the Archangel who leads God's troops into battle, and who clashes with Satan himself. Milton says: "the sword / Of Michael from the armory of God / Was giv'n him tempered so, that neither keen / Nor solid might resist that edge" (VI, 320–23). Michael slices Satan's sword easily with it, and then cuts right into the Fiend himself, yet "The girding sword, with discontinuous wound / Passed through him; but th' ethereal substance closed / Not long divisible" (VI, 328–331), which may have given Pullman some ideas about how to describe cutting into other worlds. Also, when one considers how Will's fingers are cut off and simply won't stop bleeding, the explanation might be that the knife has cut not only his body but also his spirit and his ghost, each of which might have some role to play in the processes of physical healing.

That Compass

Everyone knows that the phrase "His Dark Materials" came from Milton, but not as many know that the American title of Book I, *The Golden Compass* is also from Milton. The Son is creating the world we inhabit, at God's behest, and in carrying out the task, "He took the golden compasses, prepared / In God's eternal store, to circumscribe / This universe, and all created things" (VII, 225–27). This is not the alethiometer as a device, it is just the phrase that was used for the title, but it's hardly an accident that it is in Milton.

The Sons of God

Enough already? Not quite. The juiciest bit of Pullman's story is drawn from a very strange passage in the Bible, from Genesis 6:1–4:

> When men began to multiply on the face of the land and daughters were born to them, the sons of God saw that the daughters of man were so fair. And they took as their wives any they chose. Then the

Lord said, "My Spirit shall not abide in man forever, for he is flesh: his days shall be 120 years." The Nephilim were on the earth in those days, and also afterward, when the sons of God came in to the daughters of man and they bore children to them. These were the mighty men who were of old, the men of renown.

Weird, huh? I never heard a sermon on this passage. One wonders what a preacher would convey as the moral message here. The Bible proper doesn't say much more about this little episode, but what happens next is that the people turn away from God and become wicked, and then God slays them all in a flood—I think you've heard about that part. But more than a few people have scratched their heads at this passage. What's up with the "sons of God" doing the dirty deed with the "daughters of men." If you're curious, there is a great deal more about this obscure part of world history in the Apocryphal writings, but for now what's important is that Milton takes up and explains all this stuff. In Book XI, lines 556–715 (I know you never made it that far in high school), Michael has been sent to kick Adam out of the Garden of Eden, but he consoles Adam by showing him all of the future, including the salvation of humanity by the Son of God (Michael does not mention Pullman's novel to Adam, for some reason, but then, I guess it's just a sketch of the future, not the details).

Milton explains this odd passage from Genesis by expanding it. The world was pastoral and good, Michael says, but somewhere another angel was up to something naughty, deep in a cave, pounding on an iron forge, "Laboring, two massy clods of iron and brass / Had melted . . . the liquid ore he drained / Into fit molds prepared; from which he formed / First his own tools; then, what else might be wrought." (XI, 565–573). In Greek mythology, this naughty fellow is called Hephaestus, while the Romans called him Vulcan. This naughty angel heads down to the world of human beings with a troop of followers and teaches the humans metal craft, including how to make weapons and to adorn themselves with jewelry made of fine metals.

It's pretty much all downhill from there. The human race in intercourse with these lusty angels make war, and build their cities, and they forget about God as they fall into what Michael calls "effeminate slackness." Basically, when all is said and done, the "sons of God" and the "daughters of men" have created a whole race of giants who are violent and very difficult to feed. These are "the mighty men of old" from Genesis, and Michael describes them as "Destroyers rightlier called and plagues of men" (XI, 697).

Pullman knows this story from Milton, but he also has studied the writings on this strange episode from the *Pseudepigrapha*, which is a name given to various ancient writings in the Biblical style (often held in esteem and given some degree of authority). Important among these writings are three apocalyptic writings called First, Second, and Third Enoch, and also Second and Third Baruch. Pullman draws heavily from these writings for his content. For example, the idea that Enoch, the seventh generation from Adam, became an angel renamed Metatron comes from Chapters 3–4 of Thuird Enoch.[2] There's a great deal more from these apocryphal writings that Pullman uses for his story, but for the moment, the important event comes when an angel with the interesting name of Azazel (which is Hebrew for "scapegoat") takes a notion to pay the earth a visit:

> In those days, when the children of man had multiplied, it happened that there were born unto them handsome and beautiful daughters. And the angels, the children of heaven, saw them and desired them; and they said to one another, "Come, let us choose wives for ourselves from among the daughters of man and beget us children . . . And they took wives unto themselves, and everyone respectively chose one woman for himself, and they began to go unto them. And they taught them magical medicine, incantations, the cutting of roots, and taught them about plants. (First Enoch 6:1–2, 7:1–2)

Here we find the origin of the witches of Lyra's world, and the reason they live so long (they are the daughters of angels), and what sort of magic they can perform. But there's more. "And Azazel taught the people the art of making swords and knives, and shields, and breastplates, and . . . decorations" (8:1). For disclosing the arts of metallurgy to the humans, Azazel is punished by God, who tells Raphael: "Bind Azazel hand and foot and throw him into the darkness!" (10:4) Enoch says to Azazel: "There will not be peace unto you; a grave judgment has come upon you. They will put you in bonds, and you will not have an opportunity for rest and supplication, because you have taught injustice, and because you have

---

[2] See *The Old Testament Pseudepigrapha*, two volumes (Doubleday, 1983), Volume 1, pp. 257–58.

shown the people deeds of shame, injustice, and sin" (13:1-2). Milton also mentions Azazel by name, and designates him as the standard bearer for Lucifer's army.

So, putting two and two together, here is what you get: the model for Asriel is Azazel. Lord Asriel is not a man, he's an angel who has chosen a wife from among the daughters of men, namely Mrs. Coulter. The enmity between Enoch (Metatron) and Asriel goes back to the time when Asriel was cast down and bound. The angel of light in Pullman is not Lucifer but is Xaphania, and she and Asriel have planned this new challenge to the old order, and have done so by repeating the "sin" of Genesis 6:1–4. The witches have a prophecy about Lyra because they are the surviving female offspring of the fallen angels who retain the wisdom they learned back in the days before the first war in heaven. They know that the sign of the new challenge will come when one of the defeated angels has a daughter by one of the daughters of men. This hypothesis about Asriel is confirmed when the witch queen Ruta Skadi describes her visit to Lord Asriel's Adamant Tower, raised to make war with heaven:

> How has he done this? I think he must have been preparing this for a long time, for eons. He was preparing this before we were born, sisters, even though he is so much younger . . . But how can that be? I don't know I can't understand. I think he commands time, he makes it run fast or slow according to his will. (AS, p. 270)

The queen's erotic desire is inflamed and she does with Lord Asriel what the witches did back in Genesis. The suggestion that witches are the daughters of the angels is, as far as I can tell, Pullman's invention, but it nicely draws the story together. There is a great deal of crypto-matriarchy being suggested here, which may be the reason that instead of Lucifer, the principal among the fallen angels is female. And perhaps the angel Xaphania is really in charge of all this rebellion. Her name is probably taken from the *Pseudepigrapha* also, from the Apocalypse of Zephania, which is (among other things) a study in angelology and their orders and places in the heavenly city.

The discussion of Pullman's use of sources beyond Milton could go on forever, so I bring in the *Pseudepigrapha* here more to suggest where you might look for more information. I mention it only to the degree that this information solves some riddles that remain from the trilogy. Pullman never really explains that Asriel is an angel who has succeeded in breaking his ancient bonds and condensing into a substantial form such that the re-enactment of the sin of Genesis 6 is now possible again. Pullman never tells us why Lyra is so special, or what gives her the standing to play the part of Eve again, but the key is Genesis 6. Pullman gives us enough clues to work out who Asriel is, if we are willing to follow the trail. And obviously, this tells us a bit about Mrs. Coulter too. She is irresistible to the angels, whether Asriel or Metatron. But why? She is not Eve, after all.

A hint is to be found when Milton, describing Eve as she serves supper to Adam and Raphael in paradise, says, tantalizingly: "Meanwhile at table Eve / Ministered naked, and their flowing cups / with pleasant liquors crowned. O innocence / Deserving Paradise! If ever, then, / Then had the Sons of God excuse to have been / Enamored at that sight; but in those hearts / Love unlibidinous reigned . . ." To paraphrase a bit, here is Eve without so much as a fig leaf, pouring a righteous single malt for Adam and Raphael, and they don't even lust after her, *but Milton does.* He is sitting there thinking to himself "those idiots, there is *womanhood itself* right in front of you, and you're just drinking and chatting!"

Beyond Good and Evil

As interesting as it is, none of this source material is philosophy, *per se.* It's important to look at some of it so that we understand what sort of dark materials Pullman is working with, but until the materials are placed in some sort of order, there is really nothing more here than a lot of images and ideas. The more I have read into Pullman's sources, the more I have become convinced that our man Pullman has intentionally modeled a number of his characters on types that are "beyond good and evil." It's not the fact that they are angels or children or men and women that is crucial; it is how these characters understand morality as a set of conventions that they might or might not choose to believe. This is the famous idea (and book title) belonging to Friedrich Nietzsche (1844–1900). This little guy was withdrawn, very quiet, and a profoundly tortured soul. He wrote like it was his personal calling to cast thunderbolts from the clouds at every conventional value or traditional practice.

Nietzsche has been dead for over a hundred years, but he still makes religious people (and a lot of non-religious ones) very nervous. He was most notorious for having proclaimed that "God is dead." In Book III of the trilogy, Mrs. Coulter, confronts Father MacPhail (President of the Consistorial Court of Discipline) with the same idea, in words quite similar to a famous passage by Nietzsche. Father MacPhail says: "There are some people who claim that God is dead already. Presumably Asriel is not one of those, if he retains the ambition to kill him." To this, Mrs. Coulter replies; "Well, where is God, if he's alive? And why doesn't he speak anymore? . . .Where is he now? Is he still alive, at some inconceivable age, decrepit and demented, unable to think or act or speak and unable to die, a rotten hulk? And if that is his condition, wouldn't it be the most merciful thing, the truest proof of our love of God, to seek him out and give him the gift of death?" (AS, pp. 293–94)

This passage clinches the deal. It's pure Nietzsche, and Pullman intends us to know this. He built into Mrs. Coulter's discourse not only words and dialectical twists exactly in the style of Nietzsche, but also included a description of how Nietzsche spent the last twelve years of his own short life—"decrepit and demented, unable to think, act, speak, and unable to die." I do believe I discern Pullman's desire to go back in time and free Nietzsche from this suffering. And Nietzsche famously spoke of "Free Death," the heroic choice to die at the time of one's own choosing, just a few pages away from his most infamous passage about the death of God in his book *The Gay Science*. There's no question in my mind that Pullman intends us to understand Mrs. Coulter in association with Nietzsche. He even adds, after Mrs. Coulter has challenged Father MacPhail, that "Mrs. Coulter felt a calm exhilaration as she spoke. She wondered if she'd ever get out alive; but it was intoxicating, to speak like this to this man" (AS, p. 294).

Once it's clear that Pullman intends his readers to see an engagement with Nietzsche's philosophy in his writing, other things about the story fall into place. He also intends us to see the characters of Lyra and Will, along with those of Asriel, Mrs. Coulter, John Perry, and Metatron, as carrying out a cosmic battle that is "beyond good and evil," which is to say, they employ a kind of judgment that is incomprehensible from within conventional moral standards and ideas. None of these characters feels the least bit bound either by conventional morals or by any kind of ordinary human emotion. They are "overmen," or in German, *Übermenschen*.

This doctrine of Nietzsche's has caused a lot of problems historically—the idea that a race of men will appear that supersedes and replaces humankind as we now know it. To such beings as these, we seem like insects, almost brainless slaves to everything that is weak and contemptible. Overmen don't live by our standards, and they ought not, since our morality is devised by the weakest, most envious and vile among us—in Nietzsche's word, "Christians." Pullman stays away from any serious critique of Jesus or Christ, but this only reinforces Nietzsche's distinction between The Church, which was the invention of St. Paul, whom Nietzsche detests, and Jesus, whom Nietzsche admires as one who was too good for this world. Pullman steers clear of anything praiseworthy in the history of conventional religion and concentrates on the aspects of religious history that Nietzsche roundly condemned.

I have discussed Asriel and Metatron already. They are neither villains nor heroes; they are contending forces more powerful than we humans can understand. Their concerns are beyond our ken, and our moral judgments regarding them are of no interest to them. If you don't especially like Lord Asriel, who mercilessly murders Roger the kitchen boy so that he can re-establish his forges and smithies in an empty world, well, you aren't *supposed* to like him, and what's that to him? If Metatron seems to be a lecherous old angel, he isn't even slightly ashamed of it. You and your silly little moral qualms can go to blazes, for all they care.

What about our favorite children, Will and Lyra? How does a child exist beyond conventional morality, and become stronger than all others, in spite of having conventional morality constantly thrust upon him or her? First, Pullman is careful to give the children extraordinary genes (and we have already noted Lyra's genealogy), but then he also devises childhood settings that deprive them of ordinary experiences. He suggests, by way of his plot choices, that the paths that lead to a girl version and a boy version of the "overman" are quite different. On the "boy" side, Will is driven by *will* –not the will to power in the conventional sense, but the will to fulfill his fate, to take up his father's mantel of warrior and shaman, and to exist beyond the limitations of ordinary men by the strength of his will. The Freudian implications of his bearing a "subtle knife" are obvious enough, I suppose, as are those of fighting with one's own father in the dark. There is nothing subtle about the positioning of Will's mother between him and his father. Apparently the boy doesn't evade the oedipal struggle just by being beyond good and evil. As with Nietzsche's overman, Will simultaneously detests violence and uses it without a moment's hesitation. The boy rises to overman by means of his will, it seems.

The girl rises to overwoman by more complex pathways. Pullman names her "Lyra" to emphasize the stark contrast between truth and lies. There is a difference, Nietzsche says, between "truth-and-falsehood," which is a conventional, intellectual idea (driven by a simple-minded logic and infected with conventional judgments about good and bad), and between "truth-and-lies," which is a contest of imaginations. In all cases we try to survive by inventing simulations, but

> this is the means by which the weaker, less robust individuals preserve themselves . . . In man [not overman], this art of simulation reaches its peak: here deception, flattery, lying and cheating, talking behind the back, living in borrowed splendor, being masked, the disguise of convention, acting a role before others and before oneself –in short, the constant fluttering around the single flame of vanity is so much the rule and the law that *almost* nothing is more incomprehensible than how an honest and pure urge for truth could make its appearance among men. ("On Truth and Lies in an Extra-moral Sense," *The Portable Nietzsche*, p. 43)

But Lyra will overcome this dilemma. Here, in a nutshell, is the tension Mrs. Coulter has to face as she tries to ascend from the fetters of convention and the Church to her genuine nature, which is beyond all that. It is difficult. Lyra, on the other hand, is given, by her nature, a perfect command of both truth and lies. Both require practice, but both arts come easily to Lyra: the lies come not by way of imagination (Pullman makes a point of saying she is unimaginative), but simply because Lyra feels no constraint; and truth comes to her by way of a technology of symbols. As Nietzsche puts it: "What, then, is truth? A mobile army of metaphors, metonyms, and anthropomorphisms" (p. 46). In short, truth is an alethiometer. It is important to remember here that vivid imagination is not to blame for Lyra's lies. Xaphania's later teaching about the value of imagination, and the difficulty of learning to travel by its means, is at stake here.

Thus, Lyra tells the truth just as she lies: from beyond conventional morality. By analogy, Will is the true despiser of violence but finds himself continually required to engage in it to preserve his own unalterable purpose. His violence is not the violence of blind followers or of those who oppress others and call the situation "peace" or "order" or "law." Thus, one of the more peculiar passages in the trilogy is explained. When Lyra first encounters Will in Cittàgazze, Lyra asks the alethiometer *"What is he [Will]? A friend or an enemy?* The alethiometer answered: *He is a murderer"* (SK, p. 28).

Now, I don't know about you, but if I was in Lyra's spot, I wouldn't be inclined to think of that as good news. But Pullman says, "When she saw the answer, she relaxed at once. He could find food, and show her how to reach Oxford, and those were powers that were useful, but he might still have been untrustworthy or cowardly. A murderer was a worthy companion. She felt as safe with him as she'd felt with Iorek Byrnison, the armored bear." That's it. That's pretty much the whole explanation we ever get from Pullman. There's a tiny bit of elaboration on it later in the story, but the bottom line is that Lyra trusts Will *because* Will is, like herself, operating outside of conventional, cowardly morality, where no one can be trusted. And as Nietzsche puts it, "Is it not better to fall into the hands of a murderer than into the dreams of a lustful woman?" (*Thus Spoke Zarathustra*, "Of Chastity," p. 81). There we pretty much have Nietzsche's version of the story of Will rescuing Lyra from the sleep into which Mrs. Coulter has delivered her.

But notice that Lyra's path to overwoman is not a fight, it's a decision about which boy to follow. When she does anything apart from following Will, she gets into terrible trouble and messes everything up. Will on the other hand always knows what to do, because he does what he *has* to do and nothing else. Eventually, Will even begins to tell Lyra when to use the alethiometer, and she pretty much does whatever he says. We will discover more about the overwoman later, but for now, I just want to register with you, dear reader, that this arrangement between overman and overwoman follows Nietzsche's very controversial views about women. He rather famously characterizes them as being clever liars, but the hardest pills to swallow these days are these three remarks:

1. "Everything about woman is a riddle, and everything about woman has one solution: pregnancy."

2. "The man's happiness is: I will. The woman's happiness is: He will."

3. "Are you visiting women? Don't forget your whip!"

These are all from the same section of *Thus Spoke Zarathustra* ("Of Old and Young Women") which would be worth your while to read in full, thinking all the while of Lyra and Mrs. Coulter. Uncomfortable as it may be, Pullman is following this line of thinking in Nietzsche as well. He retains the ideas of active masculine virtues and passive feminine virtues. If anything, Mrs. Coulter rather than Lyra poses a challenge to this scheme of things, which is part of the reason Mrs. Coulter is more interesting than her daughter.

Pullman has written his epic trilogy on a latticework of Nietzsche's philosophical ideas about the death of God, about the ideas of good and evil, truth and lies, the will to power, and overmen and overwomen. It is not quite right to think of him as having rewritten John Milton or the Bible or *The Chronicles of Narnia* or Tolkien's trilogy with an inverted theology. Those elements contribute to the content of Pullman's trilogy, but the ideas under consideration are pretty much Nietzsche's. Pullman has narrated what Nietzsche called the "transvaluation of all values" in the form of a fable—which is exactly what Nietzsche himself did in *Thus Spoke Zarathustra*. But Pullman's story is for children, the children of the future, after the long awaited death of God.

Pullman names Nietzsche in interviews about this subject, and the evangelical Christians have been very quick to exploit Nietzsche's "bad reputation" as a weapon against Pullman. It is less comfortable for me to contemplate the other author who attempted this, Ayn Rand. Her lead characters were beyond good and evil, and Lord Asriel bears a striking resemblance to John Galt in *Atlas Shrugged*. But in my judgment, if one has any affinity for Nietzsche at all, one does well to skip Rand and just read Nietzsche. Rand's writing and ideas are caricatures of Nietzschean ideas and lead only to narrow-minded selfishness, not to anything morally interesting. Pullman, by contrast, has far greater insight. And I don't see Pullman endorsing Nietzsche's views or advocating them. I think he is actually offering a critique of Nietzsche.

Now maybe this little journey through Nietzsche hasn't been all that much fun (as far as I can tell, Nietzsche never had fun in his life), but hold your horses for a second—Nietzsche's last act before they institutionalized him for insanity was to collapse at the sight of a horse being beaten, but I won't beat your horses, I just want them held. Pullman is not a raving Nietzschean, I promise.

In Mrs. Coulter's Cave

In Book III, Pullman has Mrs. Coulter and Lyra re-enact the mythic drama of Demeter and Persephone, in which Will, acting the part of Hades, steals Lyra (Persephone) from Mrs. Coulter (Demeter) and takes her to the underworld to be queen there. Afterwards, Mrs. Coulter is altered. She is at the mercy of the power of motherhood, and she provides several drippy (and to my mind over-written and overwrought) apologies for motherhood. It's all pretty unconvincing. This is *not* Mrs. Coulter, or at least, it isn't the Mrs. Coulter I have a crush on. Even Asriel expresses something like contempt for this new, simpering, shadow-of-the-woman-she-was. Yes, she still plays each side off against the other, but there is a change. Now Mrs. Coulter is bereft of all religiousness, which is the power of fear, and this had been a source of her mystery and strength.

I want to make two points about where Pullman goes with his wicked woman:

1. Pullman created a character so powerful he didn't know what to do with her. Demeter was a cop-out. Mrs. Coulter, he says, is what happens to woman in a world dominated by the two overmen, Metatron and Asriel. There is no way for a woman to prevail in such a world, and that leads to my second point.

2. Sending Coulter into the Abyss with Asriel and Metatron suggests to me a no-win situation for the Nietzschean overwoman. Pullman is not endorsing the world of Nietzsche and is suggesting that in such a world, the superior woman has no real place.

The most interesting path would have been to let Mrs. Coulter's character go where she naturally would have—which is to say, in a fearless novel, Mrs. Coulter prevails. Why should Lyra be such a weakness for a woman who is corruption incarnate? And with a choice between a woman who is beyond good and evil and a rival man, my money's on the woman. This is the woman who can break the subtle knife, see witches when they're invisible, torture a witch without a moment's hesitation, and have the entire Church trembling in fear. This is the woman who can even command the specters, which is to say that she even commands the abyss. Mrs. Coulter, if you must know, is the woman Milton was lusting after when he imagined Eve, the babe so righteous looking that she could seduce an angel or a man as upright as Adam. But having created her, Pullman pulls back from the edge. Having created the perfect character, the one that might have won him literary infamy, he chose to cripple her with motherhood. As far as we know, he spares Lyra that burden. So I'm not happy about Pullman's effort to weasel out of his dilemma by using the *Demeter-ex-machina* strategy. But this is not about me.

Thus Spake Pullman

So what is Pullman's "teaching?" I think many people have misunderstood his point. There are so many characters with so many variant points of view that it might be difficult to extract the genuine moral theme from the trilogy. But with a little reflection, his point becomes clear. Pullman puts his teaching into the words of Mary Malone, Serafina Pekkala, and the angel Xaphania.

Mary is the wisdom of clear-headed scientific understanding that is not the servant of dogma and not closed to spiritual realities. She is the "sister" of the witch, whose understanding of nature is intuitive rather than scientific, and the witch has also reformed the traditional ways of witches with a willingness to consider innovation and to overcome dogma as it has settled in to the society of witches. Xaphania speaks for the spiritual wisdom of the ages, and for the proper use of human imagination. All of this is offered in the final chapters of Book III. It isn't very exciting.

Pullman also provides Will's and Lyra's responses to their teaching. Will, the masculine principle, takes Mary as his friend and guide. Lyra takes Serafina as hers. In so doing, Lyra overcomes the lies, but also loses access to truth when she can no longer read the alethiometer—unless she's willing to commit a lifetime of study to the task. Pullman is saying truth isn't easy. But in the underworld she learns that truth is really narrative in form—the way to stay within the truth involves faithfulness to one's own narrative, not to a piece of technology.

Will's peculiar challenge is that of freedom and determinism. He has struggled throughout the story with whether he is determined to be a warrior by "his nature." He declares war on his fate early in Book III when he says that even if he can't choose his nature, he can choose what he does. Nietzsche has counseled that the overman is able to love his fate, but Will (and Pullman) are taking a different view. Xaphania suggests the same. But in the crucial moment, when Will has asked Xaphania what is his "task" in life, he stops her from telling him, because knowing her wisdom only perpetuates the struggle between freedom and fate. Thus, Pullman isn't saying he has a solution to the issue of freedom and fate, or of truth and lies. He is saying that even for Will and Lyra, after the crash and collapse of the world of powers beyond good and evil, still the philosophical problems remain. Pullman's advice is: truth is hard to know and knowing it takes work, and we are free to choose what we do, so long as we don't trouble ourselves over-much about questions that are beyond our ken.

Pullman places all three teachings in the viewpoints of female characters. It is very clear that Pullman regards not only wisdom, but intuition and empirical knowledge as feminine virtues. That's why the yearly meeting is Lyra's idea, not Will's. They live in different worlds, but for an hour, in the noonday sun, on midsummer's day, they might quietly seek to occupy the same time in complementary spaces.

Xaphania's teaching is of the goodness of dust, and it sounds like the Boy Scout pledge: we are supposed to be cheerful, kind, patient, and curious, and that's how we renew the life force. But in particular, Xaphania wants to redeem imagination, and traveling by its means:

> We [angels] have other ways of traveling . . . It uses the faculty of what you call imagination. But that does not mean *making things up*. It is a form of seeing. . . . Pretending is easy. This way is hard, but much truer. . . . It takes long practice, yes. You have to work. Did you think you could snap your fingers, and have it as a gift? What is worth having is worth working for. (AS, p. 443)

This is Pullman's theme, and it is equally critical of church and of state, and of any and every dogma. What he praises and advocates is not an overthrow of dogma, narrow-mindedness and fear. He teaches that it always destroys itself, falls into the Abyss under its own weight. And Nietzsche's world, which is our world, allows no place for feminine wisdom. Thus, Mrs. Coulter has no choice but to re-enact all that the collective unconscious determines her to do wherever the will to power is dominant. Pullman's interest is not in what happens to the will to power, but in what alternatives there might be. That is why he doesn't need to invert Milton, doesn't need to endorse Nietzsche, doesn't need to attack scriptural or mythic traditions, or anything of the sort. His positive suggestions may not be so startlingly new or profound, but they do have the tinge of common sense.

Incidentally, Xaphania's teaching also fulfills what I promised at the outset. Philosophy, like the travel of angels, isn't just making things up, at least not really. It requires imagination, but also a lifetime of work. But it's worth working for, and by taking the time to read thought-provoking literature, like Pullman's books, you are well on your way to learning that way of traveling.[3]

[3] I would like to thank my friend Richard L. Cohen for his help in editing this chapter.

2
One of These Gods Is Not Like the Other

RACHEL ROBISON

There's no shortage of controversy over Philip Pullman's *His Dark Materials* trilogy. The novels take a dim view of organized religion, portraying it as an institution which has power as its goal and is willing to tear the souls away from children in order to maintain that power. Even more dramatically, Lord Asriel, one of the key characters in the trilogy, embarks on a quest to kill God in order to reclaim freedom for all the persons under the deity's tyrannical rule. Critics of the series object that the novels are directed toward children; at this impressionable age, the content of the novels may cause them to reject religion and form the belief that faith in God is dangerous.

The Authority and the Christian God

What is it that leads those thinkers who believe in God to the conclusion that such a being is worthy of praise and worship? It's not just the fact that he is our creator. One can imagine a malevolent being creating a universe for the sole purpose of inflicting pain and suffering on its inhabitants. Such a creator would be the proper object of fear and possibly anger, but not worship and praise. Similarly, one could imagine a wiser being creating life in a universe in much the same way that a scientist cultivates bacteria in a petrie dish. Once the life is created, this being pays little attention to it and is completely apathetic when it comes to the well-being of the creatures he has created. Such a creator doesn't seem deserving of worship either. One might be grateful to the entity, but could not be criticized for failing to be awe-inspired in a way that properly motivates worship.

25

The reason that religious thinkers believe that God is worthy of our worship and praise is that he is a being who possesses all perfections appropriate to a God. What would such perfections be? There are certain role-based perfections that we can rule out. A perfect piece of chocolate may have a taste that is the best possible balance of bitterness and sweetness. This is not a perfection that we would expect God to have, for God is not a piece of chocolate. The perfections we would expect God to have are those perfections that are thought by philosophers and theologians to be appropriate to a God. These perfections are being all-good (omnibenevolence), all-knowing (omniscience), and all-powerful (omnipotence).

Omnibenevolence

We have seen why, in virtue of his attributes, the Christian God, if he exists, is worthy of worship and praise. But what of the God that Pullman has created? Does he have attributes that are equally worthy of worship? Let's first consider the issue of omnibenevolence. If a being is omnibenevolent, then that being has a desire to bring about the best possible state of affairs and, if possible, the being acts on this desire (as we will see, for an omnipotent being, acting on this desire will always be possible). The best possible state of affairs will be the state of affairs that is best not just for God, but for all of his creatures. If this is the case then a world without suffering in it will presumably be better than a world in which suffering occurs.

On the face of it, it seems that if a God who either created or rules over a universe is both all good and all powerful, then there should not be suffering in that universe. At first blush, one might think that a world with suffering in it is logically inconsistent with an omnibenevolent God. This problem is known by philosophers and theologians as "The Problem of Evil," and it is a problem for any God who is thought to be omnibenevolent, omniscient, and omnipotent. If suffering exists in the world, then either God desires that his creatures suffer (in which case he is not omnibenevolent), he does not have the power to prevent the suffering (in which case he is not omnipotent), or he does not know that the suffering is occurring (in which case he is not omniscient).

Let's see whether the God of the *His Dark Materials* trilogy is resistant to the problem of evil. To do this, one need only look to see whether suffering exists in Pullman's universe. We need not even finish the first chapter of the first book in the series to find what we are looking for:

> The Master took from his pocket a folded paper and laid it on the table beside the wine. He took the stopper out of a decanter containing a rich golden wine, unfolded the paper, and poured a thin stream of white powder into the decanter before crumpling the paper and throwing it into the fire. Then he took a pencil from his pocket stirred the wine until the powder had dissolved, and replaced the stopper. (*The Golden Compass*, Knopf, 2002, p. 6)

Right out of the gate, we see a trusted official of a prestigious university attempting to poison a man to prevent him from relaying information that is dangerous to the Church. And he would have gotten away with it too if it weren't for that blasted kid!

But, you might think, the master didn't succeed in his plot to kill Lord Asriel. The Authority survives the first chapter unscathed by the Problem of Evil. Perhaps. But we don't need to look very much further to see parents grieving because their children have been kidnapped, an armored bear reduced to a shadow of his former glory because his armor has been taken from him, and, perhaps the greatest suffering seen in the series, the cutting of a child from their dæmon. Doctor Cooper, who is in charge of the cutting process, describes the procedure in the following way:

> So we've developed a kind of guillotine, I suppose you could say. The blade is made of manganese and titanium alloy, and the child is placed in a compartment—like a small cabin—of alloy mesh, with the dæmon in a similar compartment connecting with it. While there is a connection, of course, the link remains. Then the blade is brought down between them, severing the link at once. (p. 273)

This description would sound grotesque enough if what Dr. Cooper and his cohorts were doing was cutting off body parts, but what he is describing is actually cutting a child away from their soul. This is an extremely painful process which ruins the lives of the children it is performed on. The suffering of poor Tony Makarios is unparalleled:

> He couldn't settle, he couldn't stay in one place; he kept asking after his dæmon, where she was, was she a coming soon, and all; and he

kept such a tight hold on that bare old piece of fish as if . . . Oh, I can't speak of it, child; but he closed his eyes and finally fell still, and that was the first time he looked peaceful, for he was like any other dead person then, with their dæmon gone in the course of nature. (p. 218)

If the Authority knows of this immense suffering that the people in his universe are experiencing and does nothing, then it seems he is either not omnibenevolent, not omnipotent, or not omniscient.

You might be thinking that it may be true that Pullman's Authority is subject to the Problem of Evil, but that in this respect the Authority and the Christian God in our non-fictional universe stand or fall together. For surely there is immense suffering in this world. People go hungry every day. Innocent people are brutally killed. Painful diseases ravage massive numbers of the populace. All of this is true. But, as we'll see, a difference remains between the trouble the Problem of Evil poses for Pullman's Authority and the trouble the problem creates for the Christian God.

There is a way to reject the conclusion that the existence of suffering in the world is logically inconsistent with God's omnibenevolence. In order to show this, thinkers construct what they call theodicies—apologies or explanations for God's actions that show that the actions in question are not inconsistent with his divine attributes. In response to the Problem of Evil, such theodicies suggest that there is something God desires to put in the world that is so good that a world which contains this thing and all of the suffering that comes with it is, in fact, the best possible world. A common suggestion for this special something is free will. Free will is so good that, even though it produces suffering, the world with free will and all its resultant suffering is the best possible world. This kind of a response carves out a place in logical space for it to be the case both that evil exists in the world and God is all-good.

This kind of a response is not available to save the God of Pullman's universe. Why? Because we actually know what the Authority's intentions are. We know that even if the Authority had the power to change the fact that people are suffering in the world, he does not have the desire to end it. In fact, through the years he has allowed clouds to gather around his citadel on the Clouded Mountain and has even delegated much of his Authority to another angel—Metatron, whom he certainly would have known did not have the best interests of others at heart. We even see Metatron attempt to kill a number of characters in the book, including Balthamos, Baruch, and perhaps Will. He sends a large, fierce angel to attack the party:

> The clouds were parting, and through the dark gap a figure was speeding down: small at first, but as it came closer second by second, the form became bigger and more imposing. He was making straight for them, with unmistakable malevolence. (*The Amber Spyglass*, Knopf, 2002, p. 29)

Pullman describes Metatron and his followers as beings that often have sinister intentions. An omniscient, omnibenevolent God would certainly not delegate his authority to such a malevolent being.

Unlike in our own world, we really do know these facts about the Authority. There are beings who actually interact with him and are aware that he has weaknesses. These facts about the Authority bar an attempt to save him from the trouble raised by the Problem of Evil. For though it may be true that a theodicy shows that an omnibenevolent God is not logically inconsistent with the existence of evil, we know that in the case of the Authority, it actually turns out to be the case that God is simply apathetic about the suffering of the creatures over which he claims authority. We have conclusive evidence that at least part of the reason that the Authority does not intervene to stop suffering is that he simply doesn't care.

We do not have the same access to the actual actions and desires of the Christian God. Theodicies show that it is at least possible that, in order to create the best possible world, it was necessary for God to create a world with some evil in it. This story allows us to hold on to, at least for the time being, God's divine attributes, including omnibenevolence.

Omniscience

Let's move on to a second attribute that the Christian God is commonly taken to have—omniscience. Is the God of Pullman's universe omniscient? I will provide at least one reason to think he is not. One puzzle that gets raised in philosophy of religion is the following: if God is omniscient, then he knows everything that can be known. This would include facts about the future. Some facts about the future are facts about the actions that agents will perform. If this is the case, then God knew before we ever performed an action that we would perform that very action. If this is the case, then we do not act freely. We cannot do other than what God knew we would do.

Consider the case of Lyra. Lyra has a destiny and all sorts of entities in the book seem to know about it. The witches certainly do. The Oblation Board tortures one of them to learn what she knows about Lyra's destiny. In her agony, she confesses:

> She is the one who came before, and you have hated her and feared her ever since! Well now, she has come again, and you failed to find her . . . She was there on Svalbard—she was with Lord Asriel, and you lost her. She escaped and she will be— (*The Subtle Knife*, Knopf, 2002, p. 39)

The witch is here referring to the "name of [Lyra's] destiny." The girl is destined to play Eve, to free all living creatures. This confession motivates Mrs. Coulter to find Lyra and coax her into a deep sleep so she can hide with her safely in a remote cave.

Not long after the Oblation Board learns the news about Lyra, the Consistorial Court of Discipline learns it as well from an alethiometer reader:

> It says that if it comes about that the child is tempted, as Eve was, then she is likely to fall. On the outcome will depend . . . everything. And if this temptation does take place, and if the child gives in, then Dust and sin will triumph. (*Amber Spyglass*, p. 68)

After learning this news, the Consistorial Court sends out an assassin, Father Gomez, to kill Lyra so that the temptation does not occur.

Of all of the entities who should take an interest in Lyra's destiny and that should act to preserve their interests in this matter, the one who seems to have the most to lose is the Authority. All the other entities learn about Lyra's destiny with very little time left to do anything about it. Lyra's destiny, if fulfilled, will bring an end to the Authority's reign. If the Authority were omniscient, he would have known long before Lyra was ever born that she would be the one to bring about the events that led to his destruction, yet he does nothing to prepare for it, let alone stop it. When she encounters him just before he disintegrates, he seems surprised by her presence.

Omnipotence

Let's now consider the third attribute that God is commonly thought to have: omnipotence. If a being is omnipotent, they have the power to do all things that are logically possible. One only has to read the description that Pullman provides of the Authority right before he disintegrates to see that he is not all powerful. Lyra and Will find the old angel inside a crystal litter, and Pullman describes their encounter with him in the following way:

> Will cut through the crystal in one movement and reached in to help the angel out. Demented and powerless, the aged being could only weep and mumble in fear and pain and misery, and he shrank away from what seemed like yet another threat. (*Amber Spyglass*, p. 410)

As soon as Will and Lyra release him from the crystal, he vanishes completely, powerless in the face of the open air. It is hard to envisage a creature farther removed from being omnipotent.

Not only does the Authority fail to possess any of the divine attributes that the Christian God possesses, Pullman's God isn't even worthy of any gratitude. As we saw above, being a creator may be enough to warrant such gratitude. The God of Pullman's universe is not even worthy of the gratitude one might feel for their creator for, as Will learns from Balthamos, the Authority was not a creator.

> The Authority, God, the Creator, the Lord, Yahweh, Adonai, the King, the Father, the Almighty—those were all names he gave himself. He was never the creator. He was an angel like ourselves—the first angel true, the most powerful, but he was formed of Dust as we are, and Dust is only a name for what happens to matter when it begins to understand itself. Matter loves matter. It seeks to know more about itself, and Dust is formed. The first angels condensed out of Dust and the Authority was the first of all. He told those that came after him that he had created them, but it was a lie. (*Amber Spyglass*, p. 32)

Let's consider the picture we now have of the Authority. He is not omnibenevolent, so he is not worthy of worship or even respect on the basis of his goodness. He allows bad things to happen and does nothing to stop them. In fact, he even participates in them, teaming up with Metatron to create a long term inquisition. He lies to the creatures he claims authority over, telling them he created them when he didn't. Far from being worthy of worship for his goodness, the behavior of the Authority is morally reprehensible. The Authority is also not worthy of worship on the basis of his omniscience. He possesses no special powers aside from being one of the strongest angels to exist early in the history of conscious matter. He must send his regents out to discover information for him, information which, if he were omniscient, he would already know. He doesn't even seem to be aware of Lyra and her destiny, though creatures far younger and less advanced than he knew about it and acted to either help Lyra or stop her. The Authority is certainly not worthy of worship on the basis of the power he possesses. All it takes is mere open air to destroy him.

We can conclude that the Authority possesses none of the attributes that make the Christian God worthy of worship. Are there other qualities he possesses that would rightly motivate worship? The only quality that seems noteworthy about him is that he was the first conscious thing. This might make him interesting and it may even make him inherently valuable. This value would be similar to the value we might find in, for example, the bones of the earliest dinosaur. We value it for the place it occupies in our history. But though we might find value in the bones, we don't worship them for being the first. The fact that the Authority was the first conscious being should not motivate worship either, unless the length of his life has given him traits that make him worthy. There is no evidence that it did. In fact, it seems that, instead of becoming wiser and more honorable, he became weaker and more corrupt.

Pullman provides us with all of the relevant information about the Authority, and at the end of the trilogy, we can see that the God of the *His Dark Materials* universe is not the proper object of worship. The belief or faith that one might have in the Authority would boil down to believing in or having faith in some guy with no admirable qualities who played no part in creation. To give one's religious devotion to such a being would be strange and even dangerous.

If we had similar intelligence related to the Christian God, it would be morally wrong for us to continue to worship him. As evidenced in *His Dark Materials,* belief in such a being could lead us to do terrible things to our fellow creatures. What would be interesting about this situation, however, is that in our world God is defined in terms of his attributes—if we learned that God was weak or corrupt or that there were things that he failed to know, that being would not be God. If at some time in the future the person we referred to as God committed a bad act, it wouldn't be the case that that being, at that moment stopped being God. The being in question was *never* God. God, by definition is incapable of such behavior. It is not possible to worship the Christian God while mistakenly worshipping some being with the attributes that the Authority has. Because of his failings, a being like the Authority could not be God.

His Dark Materials succeeds in showing that worshiping a God with the attributes of the Authority may be bad. But the Authority is a different type of being altogether from the God that philosophers and theologians discuss in our own world. Pullman has not shown that believing in or worshipping the Christian God is a bad thing.

The Magisterium

As we have seen, the scope of Pullman's attack in the *His Dark Materials* trilogy does not extend to belief in a Christian God. Let's now consider whether Pullman's attack on organized religion is more successful.

The religion practiced in Lyra's world seems to be quite similar to the Christian religion. Its Holy text is quite similar to the Bible, only with modifications relevant to the existence of dæmons. The Magisterium, like most religious institutions in our own world, is structured in such a way that the authority figures have quite a bit of power over the way the Church is run, which also gives them quite a bit of power over the lives of the members of the Church.

It may not be bad to believe in an all-good, all-knowing, all-powerful God. It is hard to find evidence, however, that such a being actually exists. Many people long for such evidence because they find the idea that such a being exists very comforting, and in many cases it gives meaning to their lives. If a religious institution purports to have such evidence, they have substantial power over those people who believe them. Religious officials may themselves actually believe they have such evidence, and, for the sake of argument, let us assume that it is even possible that in some cases they *do,* in fact, have the evidence. What is important for Pullman's critique to be successful, however, is what these institutions are willing to do with the power that this evidence gives them.

There are least two things that the Magisterium is willing to do with their power that are morally objectionable. First, they use it to suppress information that would be useful to society. They prevent society from gaining scientific knowledge that would help people understand how the universe really works because they are afraid that it might make people turn from the Church, which would diminish its power. In its private dealings, the Magisterium acknowledges the existence of Dust and of other worlds, even using this information to perform experiments on children. In its public dealings, however, the Magisterium strives to keep information about Dust and other worlds suppressed.

Do religious institutions in our world engage in the same kind of behavior? History shows us that they certainly do. The Church punished heretics who suggested that the earth moves around the sun rather than the other way around. Religious institutions continue to ignore substantial evidence in favor of evolution because such a theory undermines the story the Church wants to tell about the beginning of life in this universe.

Second, the Magisterium is willing to harm innocent people in order to advance its agenda. It is willing to cut children from their souls because they have a vague idea that the settling of Dust *might* have something to do with original sin. They're willing to kill people for information or kill people in order to prevent classified information from becoming accessible to the public. They are even willing to kill an innocent child to keep her from fulfilling her destiny.

Do religious institutions in our own world engage in this kind of behavior? Again, it seems clear that they do. Religious institutions have been willing to kill people and destroy entire cultures in an attempt to make the whole world believe as they do. They have been willing to suggest that entire groups of peaceful people are enemies in an attempt to maintain political power. Like the religious institutions in the *His Dark Materials* universe, religious institutions in our world have historically been willing to harm innocent people in an attempt to maintain their power.

Many of the moral failings that the Magisterium has are also failings that religious institutions in our own world have. So it seems that Pullman's description of the Magisterium in the trilogy is successful as an attack on religious institutions in our own world.

Pullman and His Project

His Dark Materials doesn't succeed (and perhaps Pullman didn't intend it to succeed) in showing that belief in an all-good, all-knowing, all-powerful God is bad. Pullman's Authority is not sufficiently similar to the Christian God for Pullman to be successful in making that point. The Authority is an interesting character in a very well written series, but he is nothing like the God that philosophers and theologians discuss. He is a fictional character. Though the Christian God may possibly be a work of fiction as well, he would be a very different fictional character.

Where Pullman's critique is successful, however, is in providing an imaginative and powerful illustration of the dangers of organized religion. Unlike the comparison between God and the Authority, the comparison between the religious institutions in Pullman's world and those in our own reveals a number of morally relevant similarities.

Does the fact that Pullman's work brings to light these similarities make his book series dangerous for children? I don't think so. If approached in the right way, the books can be used to teach children valuable lessons. If the God one claims to believe in is an all-good, all-knowing, all-powerful God, and the religious institution one is affiliated with condones actions that reason tells us such a being would never advise us to engage in, that gives one good reason to question the motivations of the religious institution. Far from being dangerous, it is good to teach children to critically evaluate the actions of governing bodies rather than suggesting that they follow those bodies blindly.

If God really is all-knowing, then he knew from eternity that Pullman would write *His Dark Materials* book. If you believe God is all powerful, and if he found the series objectionable or did not think it fit into his greater plan, then he could have done something to prevent the series from being published. He didn't. Perhaps these facts should lead the religious person to look for the good in Pullman's series. God did.

3

Is Pullman Corrupting the Young?

ABROL FAIRWEATHER

In 399 B.C., Socrates was put to death for corrupting the young, and for not believing in the gods revered by his fellow Athenians. The latter charge, impiety, was the cornerstone of securing the former charge of corrupting the young. Surprisingly, 2,400 years later, Philip Pullman finds himself responding to similar charges, although in the court of public opinion rather than a court of law.

Amidst astonishing world-wide success, Pullman's *His Dark Materials* has managed to stir quite a controversy over the purportedly anti-religious message and 'sinister agenda' conveyed to a young following. Fortunately, unlike Socrates, Pullman is not fighting for his very life in court. *His Dark Materials* was, however, one of the top five most challenged books in the United States in 2007 as reported by the American Library Association, all for "Religious Viewpoint."

The religious controversy sparked by Pullman's trilogy is a mixed bag. On one hand, the fact that Pullman is not facing a trial like Socrates is a testament to our progress in the protection of fundamental freedoms and human rights. On the other hand, it shows that vestiges of Socrates's problem are still with us.

One tyrannical aspect of the Authority, the primary antagonist in Pullman's trilogy, is the suppression of ideas that question the absolute authority of the Authority. In his public response, Pullman delights in the fortuitous irony of endeavors to suppress his writing by the Catholic Church and other religious groups, when that is one of the primary evils of which his writing warns. While it's difficult not to appreciate the irony, Pullman's strong response to his religious critics has furthered their fury. Pullman's ongoing public response is nuanced, passionate, harsh, and often insightful, but neither conciliatory nor polite to the offended parties. On the other side of the coin, religious groups continue to raise deep concerns about the author of *His Dark Materials*, the spiritual bankruptcy of his trilogy, and the danger of exposing our children to either. Socrates may be smiling right about now.

The richness and complexity of *His Dark Materials* opens a number of directions for Pullman's defenders. There is his inveterate dislike of C.S Lewis's *Chronicles of Narnia*, which Pullman has called "a peevish blend of racist, misogynistic, and reactionary prejudice" (BBC interview, 16th October, 2005). There is the clear influence of Milton, many references to Blake, and even to quantum physics. There is also the powerful presence of existentialism and Friedrich Nietzsche.

The legal challenge to *His Dark Materials* has not succeeded and is unlikely to succeed. However, once we grant that Pullman's trilogy counts as legally protected speech, there might still be moral objections to it. There are plenty of human activities that are lawful, but morally problematic: adultery, hate speech, and many cases of lying. These actions will often pass legal muster, but will also often be deemed morally deficient. Legality and morality are two different things. In light of this distinction, the concerned parties (in the United States) will note that simple appeals to the First Amendment are not sufficient to put the moral basis of the religious concern to rest. *His Dark Materials* may raise a host of moral concerns, even if its author is protected by rights to freedom of expression.

Supporters of *His Dark Materials* may request a clarification from his religious detractors: What, exactly, *is* the moral objection? It can be seen as a combination of special features of Pullman's readership, and special features of the content of his message. The trilogy is written for and marketed to children. In J.S Mill's classic defense of individual freedoms in *On Liberty*, children are not granted the full range of freedoms enjoyed by adults. Unlike adults, children are yet to achieve "the maturity of their faculties . . . to guide their own improvement by conviction or persuasion." Because children cannot yet conduct "experiments in living" and "pursue their own good in their own way," others may rightfully decide for them until they reach the maturity of their faculties.

The very reason for which Mill restricts full political liberties for children speaks to their increased vulnerability to psychologically forceful content. Adults with a fully formed (though hopefully evolving) sense of identity have more effective resources to defend themselves against affronts to their dignity as persons. They can offer reasons and arguments to contrary, and maintain confidence in their self worth in the face of even the most disparaging criticism. Children, still in the midst of forming their sense of identity, lack these essential defenses, leaving their nascent identities easier victims to personally threatening messages.

Moving from features of Pullman's readership to features of his message, we must appreciate the influence of the provocative German philosopher Friedrich Nietzsche. Nietzsche is the author of the infamous line "God is dead."[1] He says not only that "God is dead", but that "we have killed him." Much of the religious concern has its origin in the Nietzscheanism lurking between the lines of *His Dark Materials*, perhaps at the forefront of its author's mind, and which reaches the vulnerable ears of eager childhood readers. The clear link between Authority and the God of the Abrahamic monotheisms, and the central plot theme of Will, Lyra, and Lord Asriel to kill the Authority suggest "killing god" as the central message of the trilogy. This is certainly the message his religious readers have seized upon as the ground of their grave concerns.

A provocative statement of Pullman's in the *Sydney Morning Herald* (13th December, 2003) sparked an Internet frenzy that quickly led to claims about the sinister agenda lurking between the lines of *His Dark Materials*. Pullman is here on record saying, "My books are about killing God," amplifying an earlier statement in the *Washington Post* that "I'm trying to undermine the basis of Christian belief." These public comments lead to a highly effective and widely disseminated chain-email attributing to Pullman the more alarming claim that "The purpose of my books is to kill God in the minds of children." This particular wording has never been confirmed, but has gained considerable traction in religious circles, and has ultimately led to Pullman's branding, by Peter Hitchens, as "the most dangerous author in Britain." At the core of Pullman's religious disenchantment is not that theism is false on matters of fact, as an adherent of evolution might complain to an adherent of creationism, but that it "makes doing evil feel so good." Theism is not

---

[1] This line is often attributed to the Prologue of *Thus Spoke Zarathustra*, where the death of God is indeed pronounced. However, the first occurrence is in *The Gay Science,* section 108, and most famously from the mouth of the madman in section 125.

just false, it is harmful. Nietzsche would certainly be a Pullman supporter on this point.

Putting these points together, the message of *His Dark Materials* is perceived as more than a "God is dead" ideology, but rather an exhortation to be the killer. It is precisely the killers of God that his young readers identify with in the trilogy, who may in turn feel a sense of complicity in the act itself. The combination of Pullman's violent expression of his religious disbelief (*killing* God), the complicity of minors in killing The Authority, and a psychologically vulnerable readership constitute the hub of the moral objection.

A Special Form of Violence?

There is no established rating system for books comparable to what we have for movies, and the idea has been consistently rejected when broached. However, the way movies are rated for different age groups may help to clarify the issues. The main variables used to determine a rating from G to R for a movie include sex, nudity, drugs, and violence. While the romance between Will and Lyra may make a young reader blush, there is, of course no explicit sex. But there is some violence. If Pullman's religious critics can show that objections to *His Dark Materials* rest on the widely accepted goal of protecting children from violent content, the burden of proof may fall to Pullman's defenders.

However, since we see plenty of graphic fantasy violence in *Harry Potter, Lord of The Rings, The Chronicles of Narnia*, and countless classics for young readers, there would appear nothing exceptional about the many violent acts described in *His Dark Materials*. To ground a concern based on violent content, there must be something special about the violence in the trilogy which sets it apart from the violent content which, perhaps regrettably, children are exposed to on a regular basis. Perhaps there *is* something different about killing the Authority.

His Dark Materials is not only about killing a character of fiction, but, as Pullman himself suggests, killing the God worshipped and loved by well over a billion human beings, and undermining the basis of their spiritual life in the process. The American Psychological Association recognizes a form of violence that damages the human soul, but which does not require an overt act of violence to do so. This subtle, but deep injury to a person is called "spiritual violence," and it is particularly damaging to children. In a narrow sense, spiritual violence diminishes its victim's self worth because of his or her religion, or for failure to meet the standards of some religion. Religious condemnations of homosexuality are often cited as a paradigm case.

In a broader sense, spiritual violence targets a person's identity, their essence as an individual, and the structures that give meaning to their life, whether these are found inside or outside of religion. All too familiar examples include hate crimes and hate speech. An interesting recent argument has been made that hate speech, while in itself nothing more than sounds in the air or marks on a page, should qualify as a "tort," the legal term for an actionable injury against a person. This movement has, thus far, met the same fate as the legal challenges to *His Dark Materials*, but this failure may simply reinforce the yawning gap between legality and morality in a liberal society.

Seeing the trilogy in conjunction with Pullman's public remarks, religious readers may experience *His Dark Materials* as violence done to their identity, aggression against their essence as a person, condemnation of who they are because of their religion. Recalling Mill's point, the identity of a Christian child will be particularly susceptible to such an attack. Perhaps *His Dark Materials* should come with a warning for spiritual violence.

In the *Golden Compass*, we're introduced to a dangerous brain child of Mrs. Coulter: Intercision. This is an ingenious literary device, and a perfectly fitting example of spiritual violence. To sever the connection between a person and their dæmon denies them the formation of a complete, matured identity. Intercision is violent, leaves its victims less than fully human, and can be fatal. The moral complaint against Pullman can be expressed using his own image of what makes us fully human. *His Dark Materials* may sever a reader's connection to God by either severing an already established connection, or preventing a connection from forming in the first place. In either case, the victim is denied a complete spiritual life. If this form of spiritual deprivation is the purpose of his trilogy, Pullman's writing should be seen as alarming by his own lights. While it is a testament to his ingenuity and genius as a writer, intercision may provide religious critics with their best expression of the moral concern raised by *His Dark Materials*.

While this would be an interesting irony, Pullman's defenders would no doubt respond by arguing that religious institutions in countless cases throughout history, and no less in the present day, are the true perpetrators of spiritual violence, with atheists amongst their primary targets. Atheists have long been the victim of an intercision at the hands of religion, and the cultural institutions trapped within its yolk. Seen in this light, whatever spiritual violence there may be in the trilogy and the mind of its author, it is a form of spiritual self-defense.

While this may give Pullman's supporters some ammunition against his detractors, it sounds like returning an injury with an injury. The self defense rebuttal to the spiritual violence charge could provide some justification against the moral concern, but this comes at the cost of granting that the trilogy is injurious. This is not an ideal approach to assuaging the moral objection. A better line of defense will show that there is a constructive purpose to killing God.

It cannot be denied that *His Dark Materials* is a work of considerable spiritual depth. However, the depth of Pullman's message may work against him unless he can assuage concerns that he is pulling off an intercision against the faithful amongst his readers. The heart of the matter for our purposes is why Pullman wants to kill god. What comes next? What is ultimately accomplished? How, and if, the moral basis of the religious objection is answered rests largely on how we answer these questions. We now consider the positive, constructive purposes of atheism, rather than seeing it merely as the destruction of theism and the spiritual life it supports.

A Public Atheist?

Philip Pullman is not the only outspoken and unapologetic atheist in town. The religious outcry against *His Dark Materials* has catapulted Pullman into a small, but growing group of 'public atheists'. The renowned biologist Richard Dawkins (*The God Delusion*), cable talk show host and director Bill Maher (*Religulous*), and Christopher Hitchens (*God Is Not Great*) are high-visibility figures, each of whom has made a point of stoutly affirming his atheism. `These figures are fighting to gain public acceptability for a creed which has long been denied a storefront in the marketplace of ideas. The atheist movement is particularly strong in the United Kingdom, the British Humanist Organization purchased ads on public buses saying "There's probably no God. Now stop worrying and enjoy your life." If an ideology is denied public visibility and acceptance, its adherents are denied the right to "living truths," to use J.S. Mill's felicitous phrase. For an individual to enjoy their own good in their own way, the creed by which they live by must be allowed expression and discussion in the larger conversation that animates community life. While it ruffles some feathers, Public Atheists are claiming this fundamental right for themselves and other atheists.

The controversy over *His Dark Materials* has catapulted Pullman into the role of an important Public Atheist, but it does not address our main question, for two reasons. First, the legal right to espouse atheism is not at issue here. Our question is about the moral status of Pullman's particular brand of atheism, not his legal right to preach it or the legitimacy of the atheist movement as a whole. Furthermore, we still want to know why Pullman is so intent on killing god. While the protests over *His Dark Materials* have had the unintended consequence of placing Pullman in the rarefied company of other elite public atheists, not to mention a big bump in sales for the trilogy, our concern is about one atheist in particular, specifically about his "sinister agenda."

Before proceeding further, we should pause to consider an interpretation of *His Dark Materials* by Donna Freitas and Jason King in their 2007 book, *Killing the Imposter God*. Freitas and King actually deny that Pullman is an atheist, public or otherwise. They claim that he is rejecting a traditional monotheistic understanding of God, and the oppressive social institutions erected in God's name. They argue that Pullman is rejecting the "tyrant God," not God *per se*. This reading of Pullman would radically reconfigure the religious controversy which lies at the heart of this chapter, as well as much of the media coverage of *His Dark Materials*.

Freitas and King read Pullman not as an atheist, but rather a "panentheist." Panentheism means "all in God"; a subtle variation of "pantheism," which means "all is God." Panentheism doesn't define God as a creator separate from creation but sees creation as immanent in God itself. Traditional monotheism radically separates God from the created universe, and from mankind itself, and sees God as a rational, rule-giving authority standing over the mind of man. The traditional concept of God has Creator and creation as radically distinct entities, the latter subservient to the former. We may have something of God's nature, but we do not live where God lives, and we are virtuous when we are subservient to divine commands. Panentheism, on the other hand, places man and God in the same world.

Freitas and King read Dust as Pullman's theological successor to the transcendent, tyrannical, oppressive creator of the world, and the institutions which enforce its ideology. Dust is "the ultimate, unifying, and animating principle in the universe, . . . the 'spirit' of human beings and all matter but also the 'form' of angels." Dust is wisdom, the spiritual force immanent in the worlds of the trilogy, and is the God of *His Dark Materials* according to Freitas and King. While this keeps Pullman at odds with the Catholic Church and other mainstream religions, the panentheist interpretation has Pullman engaging in intra-religious debate over the true nature of God, rather than casting a dagger into the heart of all gods. Perhaps Pullman is redefining rather than killing God. Perhaps His Dark Materials is just a rallying cry against oppressive religious institutions, rather than an attack on religion, *per se.*

In addition to being an interesting, and in some ways persuasive, interpretation of Pullman's religious views, *Killing the Imposter God* is also of interest because Nietzsche is discussed as a significant influence on Pullman's unusual theology. While they are right to note the influence of Nietzsche on Pullman, their reading of both appears to miss the mark in some ways.

Nietzsche is not really an atheist, according to Freitas and King, but is simply rejecting an outmoded Christian God. However, Nietzsche clearly rejects not just a Christian God, but all "other worldly" ideologies. Nietzsche's concern is that placing the locus of ultimate value in a non-human deity and a world beyond our own abdicates a deep personal responsibility that comes with human freedom. If God is the creator of values, the deepest act of human freedom is rendered obsolete, pointless, already achieved. For Nietzsche, the highest purpose in human life is to create and live in light of values of one's own making. This is to be truly an individual. The heart of Nietzsche's concerns is that God stymies true individuality. Anything that does *this*, whether religious or not, will earn Nietzsche's contempt. Nietzsche's concerns clearly go further than authoritarian religious institutions.

Freitas and King tell us that Pullman, like Nietzsche, only rejects authoritarian religious institutions, "tyrant Gods." Killing the Authority is killing this God, not every God. If their reading is correct, then it's incorrect to categorize Pullman as an all-out atheist. Admittedly, their panentheist, non-atheist, interpretation provides an interesting perspective on *His Dark Materials* that would seem to undercut the religious controversy in which Pullman is embroiled. However, like their reading of Nietzsche, I think more is going on in killing the Authority than objecting to oppressive religious institutions, and for similar reasons.

The interpretation of Pullman in *Killing the Imposter God* essentially deifies Dust. But, one thing we don't want Dust to do is to simply replace the overreaching moral authority of the Authority. This would be like reading Nietszsche's Overman, the creator of values, as replacing one "other worldly" religion with another, when Nietzsche's problem is with "other worldly" ideologies as such. Likewise, Authority is not only an oppressive social institution; it deprives individuals of the essential purpose of human freedom. The Authority denies the most important creative act in human life by relegating the meaning of individual lives to a logic of discovery, rather than a logic of creation. It's not clear that panentheism does any better on this score, if the values we ought to live by still lie fully formed in God, whether a God of this world or of another world.

It would be rash to conclude that the panentheist interpretation is wrong, although it certainly appears that Pullman wants to be an atheist. Perhaps we should just let him be one. In either case, what does seem clear is that, whether Pullman is an atheist or a panentheist, Dust should not play the same role in defining the values individuals should live by as does the Authority. Dust would then be no friend of freedom.

What Is Freedom For?

Freedom is central to the purpose of killing God for both Nietzsche and Pullman, but how exactly are the two connected? In different ways, both Will and Lyra exercise freedom at critical junctures in the trilogy. A fairly obvious connection between the Authority and freedom in *His Dark Materials* is that the former impedes the latter, to the point of threatening its extinction. Nietzsche recognizes a similar threatening connection between God and freedom, but he also describes the birth of a new freedom that is achieved by killing God. Here, Nietzsche tells us what freedom is for, and hence presents killing God as a constructive act. Perhaps Pullman's full message about the connection between freedom and the Authority has the mark of Nietzsche on this critical point. The moral concern raised at the outset of this paper now comes down to the connection between killing God and freedom.

What exactly is freedom? One of many strands in the history of theorizing about the nature of freedom is the distinction between Negative Freedom and Positive Freedom. To possess negative freedom is to be "free from"—free from obstacles, barriers, and strong constraints on the exercise of autonomy. We lack negative freedom when some significant, contrary force impedes the natural operation of the human will; we are unable to act as we choose to because something outside of us resists the power of our will.

To possess positive freedom is to be self-directed, to act in such a way as to take control of one's life, and realize one's fundamental purposes. Positive freedom is what we are free for, or what we are able to actually do. Freedom here moves us toward its positive aim, end, or goal. Negative liberty is typically lost by the interference of something external to the agent of action, whereas positive freedom is often abdicated by the agent himself. Complete freedom is to possess negative freedom and to exercise positive freedom.

The Authority clearly constitutes a barrier and constraint on agency and autonomy, and thus undermines negative freedom. By implication, the Authority also undermines positive freedom because the former is necessary for the latter. However, restoring negative liberty by killing the Authority achieves only a necessary, but not sufficient, condition for exercising positive freedom. Killing the Authority is thus not itself the realization of full freedom. We should not diminish the importance of this aspect of Pullman's message, for many have suffered, and continue to suffer diminished negative freedom at the hands of God. However, the full message of freedom will include some conception of positive freedom. This tells us what freedom is for, and I suggest, it gives us the key to answering the religious concern, or seeing that it cannot be answered.

Assuming we are at no significant loss of in terms of negative freedom, there are two ways in which positive freedom can be lost. We can abdicate positive freedom by falling into what Sartre calls "bad faith." This includes (but is not limited to) believing that one's fate is determined, that we are subject to, rather than being the creator of, the force that drives our life. Positive freedom may also simply remain unactualized, dormant, a mere possibility. If one is deeply indecisive or non-committal, or suffers from some kindred anemic condition of the will, our life will not be robustly self-directed. Kierkegaard discusses this way of losing oneself in *Either/Or*, when Judge William warns us not to lose sight of "the headway" that time itself is making when we linger too long in the moment of decision.[2]

In both cases, we fail to choose in a robust way, and are not meaningfully directing our own lives. To achieve positive freedom, we need a robust commitment to a motivating value, principle or aim. But, to avoid bad faith, we must resist a commitment which denies our responsibility for freely making the commitment in the first place. Our life aim is what it is because we have willed it to be so. To have no principle of action, to choose nothing, is to be stuck in nihilism. Achieving full freedom requires avoiding nihilism without falling into bad faith.

Killing the Authority could undermine positive freedom in the latter sense, if we are left without a successor system of values. This is often a concern raised about atheism; it leaves us with nothing to care about, and thus deprives us of full freedom. The loss of freedom to nihilism is a concern Pullman must address if he wants to kill God, but preserve positive freedom. However, if a successor system of values is determined by the pantheistic reading of Pullman's would-be God, the deification of Dust, as the Pullman of *Killing The Imposter God* would have it, the threat of bad faith looms. If the answer to what values should direct our life is lying, fully formed, in the universe itself, we have really abdicated, rather than fulfilled the responsibility that comes with full freedom. The latter point is also at the heart of Nietzsche's interest in killing God. Religion threatens to stamp out deep positive freedom. Let us consider whether Nietzsche's influence on Pullman's thought can be seen at this critical juncture, and what kind of answer we ultimately get to the religious concern raised at the outset.

Nietzsche's Child and Answering the Moral Objection

One of the most compelling and concise pieces written by Nietzsche is the story of "The Three Metamorphoses", the first section of *Thus Spoke Zarathustra* directly following the famous pronouncement of God's death. Nietzsche here tells us how the camel of the spirit became a lion, and the lion finally became a child. It is fitting that, given our concern about impact of the trilogy on

---

[2] For Kierkegaard's very insightful discussion of choice and selfhood see pages 102–03 in *A Kierkegaard Anthology* (Random House, 1946).

young readers that the child represents the achievement of full freedom for Nietzsche. Nietzsche's child tells us why God must killed.

Nietzsche's spiritual allegory begins with the "camel of the spirit," the beast of burden which kneels down to bear any load placed upon it. The camel's burden is not of its own making, but yet defines the camel's purpose and highest achievement. The camel is reverent to the intriguing and powerful figure, the "Great Dragon," also called the great "thou shalt." The Great Dragon claims to encompass all possible values. No values, points or purposes for life can be thought which do not already glisten on its scales. The Great Dragon demands obedience as the ultimate authority, it stands above man as its law giver, until the Lion of the spirit kills it. The Lion makes freedom possible when it slays the great "thou shalt"; the great symbol of all external authority is the Lion's prey.

This killing is extremely important; it is man's escape from the spiritual tyranny of religion. However, it is not itself freedom, but merely its possibility. The Lion, like the Camel, is wholly dependent for its life purpose on the Great Dragon. The Lion is not creating its own way, but merely destroying the obstacle that stands in its path. Without the great the Great Dragon, neither the Camel nor the Lion would have anything to do, and thus they do not give their own purpose to life.

The Child is the final stage of the spirit. Its will is its own, not simply a response to something outside of it; the spirit of the child is *sui generis*. Nietzsche tells us that the Child may be the world's outsider because it lives outside of all existing values, but it thereby wins itself. The Child of the spirit is the epitome of positive freedom, and is only possible given the death of the Great Dragon. With the realization of this freedom, Nietzsche tells us that we achieve true individuality. For Nietzsche, the point and purpose of killing God is the deep positive freedom and individuality achieved by the Child.

Is this Pullman's message? The figure of the Great Dragon is an amazing fit with the Authority and Mrs. Coulter. Lord Asriel, Will, and Lyra would fittingly be cast as the Lion of the spirit, and the Camel is the diminished spirit of those living under the Authority. But what of Nietzsche's child? The Child is not an attack against anyone's identity or self worth, and thus is not a symbol of spiritual violence. The development of the spirit toward full freedom occurs within one person, not in aggression between many. It would be a simplification of Pullman's nuanced and diverse intellect and creativity to see his ultimate message as nothing but Nietzsche's Child. However, if it were, it does not seem to fit the bill for spiritual violence, nor would the moral objection be borne out.

Another answer to the moral objection comes as we see the connection with Nietzsche fade. Pullman gives us a different way to think about positive freedom in the Republic Of Heaven. This not only replaces the religious ideal of the Kingdom of Heaven, but it has a clear social/political message and applies to individuals connected to communities, not isolated individuals. Nietzsche's message is far more individualistic, and may raise real concerns if large groups of people were to live out the Nietzschean ideal. Pullman may be radical, but he does not appear radically Nietzschean at this point.

Pullman invites his critics to recall the virtues that triumph in the trilogy: courage, compassion, love, kindness, intellectual curiosity.[3] These values do not stand outside of all existing values like Nietzsche's Child, nor do they represent a corrupting, concerning ideology for young people. The moral basis of the religious challenge to *His Dark Materials* is severely deflated at this point. The message of the trilogy is, at bottom, neither sinister, harmful to children, nor at odds with the moral core of many religions. At this point, Pullman's religious critics are left grasping for straws in the attempt to locate what we should find so objectionable.

There will, no doubt, be some that continue to criticize Pullman for using provocative images and ruffling religious feathers. Fortunately, we have laws on the books protecting our right to do that, and our freedom to describe our own good in our own way. Pullman is thus unlikely to suffer the same injustice as did Socrates. In Pullman's own words, he does have an agenda: he wants his readers to turn the pages of his books, enjoy life and exercize their intellectual curiosity. Pullman himself sums it up best:

> And I think it's time we thought about a republic of heaven instead of the kingdom of heaven. The king is dead. That's to say I believe that the king is dead. I'm an atheist. But we need heaven nonetheless, we

---

[3] See Pullman's interview with Donna Freitas on her blog, at www.donnafreitas.blogspot.com.

need all the things that heaven meant, we need joy, we need a sense of meaning and purpose in our lives, we need a connection with the universe, we need all the things that the kingdom of heaven used to promise us but failed to deliver. And, furthermore, we need it in this world where we do exist—not elsewhere, because there ain't no elsewhere. (The Republic of Heaven Speech)

4
Faith and Circumcision

WAYNE YUEN

The scene in *The Golden Compass* where Lyra finds herself about to become one of the test subjects for the silver guillotine, a device that would forever separate her and her dæmon, Pantalaimon, may be the most frightening passage in the book. The fear of a child losing her beloved animal companion at the hands of a powerful authority is heart-wrenching.

Pantalaimon is more than just a pet, he is metaphorically and literally Lyra's soul, and the silver guillotine serves as an obvious metaphor for circumcision (as well as being a metaphor for the atomic bomb). But parents who circumcise their children aren't typically blamed for their acts, yet Mrs. Coulter seems to be morally accountable for her actions. Are we inconsistently blaming Mrs. Coulter, are we inconsistently failing to chide parents who circumcise, or is there a relevant differences between the two cases? This issue is rooted to a deeper problem, Mrs. Coulter's actions and the actions of parents circumcising their children are the results of their faith. Is it morally permissible to act on beliefs without any evidence?

Circumcision is defined as the removal of the foreskin, a sheath of skin that covers the glans, on a penis. This is usually performed on infants for religious purposes, for hygienic purposes, or both. But are these reasons good enough to justify the removal of part of a person's body?

The Case Against Circumcision

In terms of hygiene, a foreskin is not particularly dirty, but rather it can trap dirt and bacteria, against the head of the penis. The removal of the foreskin makes keeping the penis clean easier. However, keeping the penis clean is not particularly difficult with a foreskin, one simply needs to pull back the foreskin and clean the glans and foreskin on a regular basis. Teaching children to have good hygiene is part of raising a child, and this is simply one more piece of information that needs to be passed along to boys who are uncircumcised. The alternative is to simply forego educating the child, and remove the foreskin altogether. This is a rather odd solution to the problem of hygiene, and would be akin to removing every other tooth of a child so one would not have to teach the child to floss.

A slightly more profound reason for circumcision is that it may help prevent HIV infection. Although the research is not conclusive, the leading theory is that the foreskin contains less keratin than normal skin cells, making it easier to be infected by HIV, as well as creating a pocket between the glans and the foreskin for the virus to exist in longer and increase the chance of infection. However, there are much more effective ways of combating HIV infection than circumcision, namely condoms and other barriers that block HIV from being transmitted not only to males, but to females as well. Educating children that it is not only for their own safety but also for the safety of their partner, whom they ideally love and respect, that they practice safe sex is far more effective of a strategy against HIV infection.

But even if this is the case, one might be tempted to circumcise their child simply to prevent the off-chance of HIV infection or bacterial infection. Yet the risk of complications with any medical procedure should be taken into account as well. In the US, complications that arise with circumcision may be as low as 0.2 percent or as high as two percent. The most common complication would be excessive bleeding and infection. Staph infections, which are not at all uncommon in hospitals, have been reported in some cases.[1] The off-chance that a child will suffer a bacterial infection is repetitiously replaced with the off chance that a child will suffer a bacterial infection.

Lord Asriel makes a similar comment about the oddness of this solution, when he recalls the precedence of castration:

---

[1] D.M. Nguyen, E. Bancroft, L. Mascola, et al. Risk Factors for Neonatal Methicillinresistant Staphylococcus Aureus Infection in a Well-Infant Nursery. *Infect Control Hosp Epidemiol.* 28 (2007), pp. 406–411.

the church wouldn't flinch at the idea of a little cut, you see. There was a precedent. And this would be so much more hygienic than the old methods, when they didn't have anesthetics or sterile bandages or proper nursing care. It would be gentle by comparison.[2]

It may be that circumcision has improved over the years, but that doesn't make it any more necessary for it to be done. The American Academy of Pediatrics published a statement in 1999, and reaffirmed it in 2005 stating, "Existing scientific evidence demonstrates potential medical benefits of newborn male circumcision; however, these data are not sufficient to recommend routine neonatal circumcision."[3] Without potential medical benefits and a host of potential harms, circumcision could be properly described as mutilation, a procedure that destroys a part of the body with virtually no benefit.

Tony Makarios, who was a victim of the guillotine, became essentially a zombie when he was separated from his dæmon. Shortly after Lyra finds him and returns to her camp, Tony dies, apparently from the procedure. In 1998, a Cleveland Ohio boy died when a surgery was performed on the child to repair damage caused to the boy's urethra after a botched circumcision. The boy had an adverse reaction to the anesthesia and never regained consciousness. Had the boy not had the circumcision, he would have not needed the subsequent surgery which cost him his life.[4]

Perhaps the most problematic aspect of circumcision is that it is done without consent of the patient. Proxy parental consent is used in place of the patient's consent because in all cases involving infants and children, they may not be rational enough to decide what is best for themselves. Most infants and children would probably refuse immunizations and going to the dentist, on the grounds that they didn't like it. However, as parents we intercede and say that this is better for them in the long run, a small amount of pain now to prevent a great deal of potential future pain. With circumcision, there is no great deal of future pain that is being prevented, only possible pain that could be prevented in other ways. Worse, there is the potential loss of future pleasure as

---

[3] Task force on Circumcision. American Academy of Pediatrics: Circumcision Policy Statement. *Pediatrics* 103:3 (March 1999), pp. 686–693. http://aappolicy.aap-publications.org/cgi/content/full/pediatrics;103/3/686.
[4] *Iowa Law Review* 85:4 (May 2000), pp. 1507–568.

foreskin contains many specialized nerve endings called stretch receptors that respond to being stretched, rolled, and pulled, the kinds of stimuli that sexual intercourse provides.

Believing in the Guillotine

However, it isn't for any of these reasons that Mrs. Coulter is cutting children with the silver guillotine. She's cutting them because she believes that the dust that settles and that prevents a person's dæmon from changing forms is original sin. If they can prevent that, by separating a person from their dæmon, then they could avoid original sin. For the most part, it is a religious belief[5] that drives Mrs. Coulter and many others to cut. Now in the course of the novels we learn that the dust is in fact not original sin, but let us place ourselves in Mrs. Coulter's position and suspend our knowledge of this. Is what Mrs. Coulter doing reasonable? This is a much more interesting question, because it mirrors the question that religious parents find themselves in today. In the Jewish tradition,[6] circumcision is a covenant with God. The Bible states:

> I will make you extremely fruitful. I will make nations of you, and kings will descend from you. I will confirm my covenant as a perpetual covenant between me and you. It will extend to your descendants after you throughout their generations. I will be your God and the God of your descendants after you. I will give the whole land of Canaan – the land where you are now residing – to you and your descendants after you as a permanent possession. I will be their God." Then God said to Abraham, "As for you, you must keep the covenantal requirement I am imposing on you and your descendants after you throughout their generations. This is my requirement that you and your descendants after you must keep: Every male among you must be circumcised. (Genesis 17:6–10)

---

[5] Many people also do it out of sheer tradition, but doing something because we've done it in the past is fallacious reasoning. Public executions, slavery, and drowning witches were done in the past as well, but this provides little justification for us to do these things today.

[6] Christian tradition grew out of the Jewish tradition, and as such, this may explain why circumcision is so common in America, but there is no circumcision requirement in the Bible for Christians. Galatians 5:6 states, "For in Christ Jesus neither circumcision nor uncircumcision carries any weight—the only thing that matters is faith working through love."

So whereas Ms. Coulter is doing it to prevent sin, Jewish orthodoxy does it as a bargain with God for his favor. These are both very good goals to achieve, assuming a religious framework.[7]

How do we determine the reasonableness of such beliefs? One possibility is that we need not determine the reasonableness of the belief at all, but rather simply hold it in good faith that the belief is true. However, there are serious problems with holding beliefs based on faith alone, especially beliefs that affect others, like circumcision, or severing a person's connection with their dæmon. W.K. Clifford in his essay titled *The Ethics of Belief* puts forth the following thought experiment: Imagine that you're an owner of a ship that is about to sail to the new world. You have some doubts about the seaworthiness of the ship, but you form a belief on faith that the ship will make it unharmed. The ship sets sail and sinks; everyone dies. It seems that the belief was an irresponsible belief. Even if the ship had made it across the ocean safely, the ship owner would have acted in an irresponsible manner. Clifford says, "It is wrong always, everywhere and for everyone to believe anything upon insufficient evidence."[8] Instead what we must do is investigate our beliefs so that we can come upon sufficient evidence for accepting or rejecting our belief.

Investigation is precisely what Mrs. Coulter is attempting to do. She is investigating her belief about the connection between dust and original sin through experimentation. Severing the link between child and dæmon, and observing what happens to them, Mrs. Coulter hopes that she can learn to sever the link correctly, freeing people from sin and not turning them into zombies at the same time. It is the methodology of her investigation, the utilization of non-consensual persons, that one can find moral fault in, not her desire to learn the truth about dust, or testing her hypothesis that it is original sin. Experimenting on children is fraught with moral problems, not the least of which is attempting to obtain informed rational consent from an agent who is not fully rational. In *The Golden Compass*, the children are kidnapped and experimented on against their will, compounding the wrongness of the scenario.

---

[7] An atheist would have very little justification for circumcising their children. But I would assume that even atheists would want to avoid sin, if they could do so.

[8] W.K. Clifford. *The Ethics of Belief and Other Essays* (Prometheus, 1999).

The Case for Circumcision

But let's imagine that Mrs. Coulter recruited willing volunteers and conducted the investigation morally. Let's further imagine that the guillotine is perfected so that children no longer become zombies after the procedure. In such a case, the arguments against circumcision seem minor, because the cut overwhelmingly works in the child's best interest, consequently it would be morally acceptable. Could there be other benefits that would make circumcision morally acceptable?

We've been thinking about male circumcision, since it is the most common. However, there is the equivalent procedure for females, clitoral circumcision. This should not be confused with Female Genital Mutilation (FGM), which has had much media exposure in recent years. Clitoral circumcision is the more analogous procedure for women since it only removes the clitoral hood and not the clitoris itself or other parts of female genitalia like the labia in FGM. In America, clitoral circumcision was encouraged by physicians from the late nineteenth century up through the 1970s as a treatment for women who were unable to achieve orgasm through vaginal intercourse alone. Ten percent of women found that they were able to achieve orgasm more easily after clitoral circumcision.[9] This may be a small percentage, but the number of women who would benefit from the procedure may be significantly higher due to the relatively low population of women who were actually circumcised in America, coupled with the cultural taboos surrounding sex, especially female sexuality, which would reduce the number of people who would seek medical treatment for sexual dysfunction.

For an act to be mutilation, it would need to damage or destroy a part of the body in a way so that there would be no intended benefits of the damage.[10] We normally wouldn't call amputation to save someone's life mutilation, but we would call cutting off a perfectly good foot for no particular benefit mutilation. So quite contrary to the popular notions of circumcision, male circumcision may

---

[9] Sara Webber and Toby L. Schonfeld, "Cutting History, Cutting Culture: Female Circumcision in the United States," *American Journal of Bioethics* 3.2 (2003), pp. 65–66.

[10] For a more thorough examination of the topic of mutilation, I recommend Lund-Molfese, Nicholas C. "What is Mutilation?." The American Journal of Bioethics 3.2 (2003): 64–65.

be closer to a kind of mutilation, whereas female circumcision would not be mutilation at all, since there could be some demonstrable benefit. (There are rare conditions where a male can benefit from being circumcised, such as phimosis, when the foreskin cannot retract, possibly preventing full erection and making intercourse unpleasant.)

Likewise, in the trilogy, there is at least one other demonstrable benefit besides preserving the purity of the soul. Lyra has something akin to having the connection between Pantalaimon and herself severed (more specifically stretched) so that she could leave him behind uninjured in her journey through the land of the dead where Pantalaimon could not survive. However, both female circumcision cases and the stretching case of witches and shamans in the novels, are undertaken with informed consent, typically by adults.

If male circumcision were to mirror female circumcision more closely, where males would not be circumcised unless there was a demonstrable benefit and under the direction of the person being circumcised, then there would be little to fret about. One would simply need to ask them if they are happy with their foreskin. If they were, then they could continue to keep it. If they were not, they could be circumcised. However those who have already been circumcised and are not happy about this, cannot have their foreskins restored.[11] Additionally, the potential medical benefits of circumcision, could be acquired in the future before the man becomes sexually active and is in much better position to give their informed consent.

There is one more possibility that we must consider: One might have no control over one's beliefs. David Hume argues that beliefs are nothing more than strong feelings that we have. Neither reason nor will would determine what we believe. I could not will myself to believe that an ordinary compass was actually an alethiometer. One might imagine that it's the case, but imagining something and truly believing something are very different things.

Most people have had the experience of trying to convince someone that something is correct, an attempt to change a belief. This is usually futile, until something, such as persuasive evidence or experience, is produced. Some kind of outside force, like encountering an actual panserbjørne, would be needed to change

---

[11] There are surgical foreskin "restoration" techniques and other techniques involving stretching existing skin, however none actually restore the foreskin.

the belief that there are no panserbjørnes. But with our beliefs about the soul, there can be no evidence of this sort to radically change a person's beliefs. If this is the case, then Clifford's thesis that one is irresponsible in holding uninvestigated beliefs is incorrect, since we can only hold people responsible for things that they have genuine control over. It wouldn't make sense to chide someone morally for an accident and under this analysis all beliefs are accidental.

To judge people based on the beliefs they hold, is problematic in another sense, in that there is no way for me to genuinely determine the kinds of beliefs you hold. I may be able to evaluate your actions but, as the saying goes, there is no thought police. It would be reasonable then, not to try to morally evaluate an agent's beliefs, but rather limit our judgment to actions.

Where's an Alethiometer when You Need One?

So how are we to judge the spiritual nature of the oblation that is circumcision? Lyra and Mrs. Coulter happen to be fortunate enough to meet with the divine beings themselves to find many of the fundamental answers that we cannot. Ultimately, we can say that Mrs. Coulter is incorrect in her beliefs about Dust. Since we cannot really investigate the spiritual implications of a circumcision, then either we have to take it on faith that it is spiritually beneficial, or we reject it in favor of what we can investigate, the physical effects of circumcision. On this point, reasonable people can disagree about this particular issue with no real resolution. Without an alethiometer, everybody is an equal authority on the care for our souls. Clifford's guidance here is clear, if we want to be fully responsible, we should reasonably suspend judgment on the spiritual implications of circumcision, since they lie beyond the possibility of knowledge. It is important to note that this is not the same as denying the truth of the spiritual implications.

However, there is a relevant difference between circumcision and intercision, which is the likelihood and severity of harm. While there are many possible harms that may occur from circumcision, even death, the likelihood of these occurring are all relatively small. Chances are circumcision will not adversely affect a child's life. Where circumcision may be a kind of physical mutilation of a relatively benign part of the body, intercision is a mutilation of the soul. Lyra has just cause to be suspicious of Mrs. Coulter, because the decisions she was making, although well-intentioned, were threatening Lyra's soul. On the matters that we can investigate, the stakes are much higher in *The Golden Compass* than in our world. Similarly, since there is much less at stake in the case of circumcision, we should not judge it as severely irresponsible as Mrs. Coulter's actions in *The Golden Compass*. At worst, it's as irresponsible as exposing your child to chicken pox.[12]

The difference in severity does not mean that the two cases fall into different categories of moral evaluation, that is one being right and the other being wrong. The difference between a serial killer and a murderer is severity, but both are wrong. But some acts that are morally wrong but not severely wrong should be treated differently from acts that are severely wrong. It may be wrong to lie to someone, but judging someone to be morally corrupt over an inconsequential lie, like lying about one's weight or what their favorite color is, would be inappropriate. But the conclusion is hard to deny, if we think it is wrong to intercise Pantalaimon from Lyra, then for similar reasons, we should think it wrong to circumcise foreskins from their owners.

---

[12] Many people expose their children to chicken pox for the benefit of the child, which will assuredly lead to an amount of physical discomfort, and holds risks of more severe long-term complications and even death. There is also a reasonable alternative in a vaccination which is eighty-five percent effective, although this is not without debate either, but that is outside the scope of this chapter.

PART II

Tell Them Stories. They Need the Truth. You Must Tell Them True Stories, and Everything Will Be Well, Just Tell Them Stories.

5

The Truth in Lyra's Lies

KIERA VACLAVIK

Swept along in the mounting drama which is the climax of *The Golden Compass*, it's easy to miss a classic case of narratorial hoodwinking. Asriel's plans are near completion; only one more ingredient is needed, and "it," we are told, is "drawing closer every minute."[1] The missing link is, of course, Roger, and a "*he*" rather than an "*it*," as Pullman knows full well. But the narrator covers his tracks and the suspense is maintained a little longer. Earlier in the novel, the connection between creativity and deceit is made explicit: both artists and liars, we read, must "be vague in some places and invent plausible details in others" (p. 283). It comes as no surprise, then, that Pullman has elsewhere described the storyteller as a "trickster" who "can persuade people of something that isn't true."[2]

The universe he has created is full to bursting with all manner of liars, tricksters, storytellers, and deceivers. From the Arctic foxes to the Almighty himself, almost every character—whether sympathetic or morally reprehensible—lies, deceives, or betrays at some point. The nurses at Bolvangar and Mrs. Coulter are of course at it, but so too are Lord Asriel, Will, his father, Mary Malone and Iorek Byrnison (who, Lyra informs us, "never lies"[3]).

[1] *Northern Lights* (Scholastic, 2001), p. 363.

[2] Wendy Parsons and Catriona Nicholson, "Talking to Philip Pullman: An Interview," *The Lion and the Unicorn* 23:1, p. 133.

[3] *Northern Lights*, p. 367.

Lyra's Lies

But can we believe Lyra when she asserts Iorek's truthfulness here or indeed anywhere else, given that she herself is a liar to the core? As her name suggests, storytelling (Lyra, lyre, lyric), invention, deception, trickery, and bluff are at the very heart of Lyra's character. Time and time again, attention is drawn to this aspect of her persona, with 'liar' acquiring the status of epithet as the trilogy unfolds. Perhaps the highlight of her career as trickster comes in the final part of the first volume when she maneuvers the villainous Iofur Raknison into a fight to the death with Iorek Byrnison. Having adroitly identified her adversary's Achilles' heel, Lyra poses as the dæmon which is his heart's desire and persuades him with great guile to do her bidding. Lyra's lies here save the day.

It's on the strength of this performance that Iorek Byrnison christens her Lyra Silvertongue. Just as she welcomes this designation, so she (like Pullman) proudly assumes her trickster identity in a whole range of situations. But when it's held against her—an accusation rather than an accolade—Lyra angrily denies the charge ("I en't dishonest!"[4]). Nine times out of ten such disavowals will themselves be falsehoods since the charges are usually well-grounded . . . But it's not because she's been found out that Lyra is enraged; it's because such accusations overlook her motives. Lyra's lies, deceptions, and inventions are invariably undertaken for very good reasons. True, in the early stages of the trilogy her stories are a means of showing off, imposing herself, and impressing others by inspiring awe and fear. This—and nothing more honorable—is what's going on when she tells Roger the bravado-laden tall stories about her uncle's ability to strike his enemies dead with a single glance (*Northern Lights*, pp. 46–47). Yet Lyra's lies also serve to comfort and assist others, to preserve her independence and guarantee her existence. In the circumstances in which she finds herself, lying and pretence are simply unavoidable: her various alter-egos are no mere play-acting whims but strategies upon which her life depends. And when like Lyra you're involved in world travel—traveling *between* worlds—a lie often proves more credible, and therefore more efficient and efficacious, than the truth.

---

[4] *The Subtle Knife* (Scholastic, 1998), p. 170.

What Lies Beneath

Experience repeatedly impresses the value and efficacy of lying upon both Lyra and the reader following her journey. Until, that is, she ventures into the Land of the Dead in the final volume of the trilogy. It's here that Lyra the liar is most visible and, in all senses of the term, most exposed. For the umpteenth time, Lyra embarks upon an elaborate fiction in order to get round the obstacle she faces. This time, however, there's no triumph. Far from it. This time her efforts elicit physical attack and verbal abuse:

> . . . the harpy was flying at them again and screaming and screaming in rage and hatred:
>
> '*Liar! Liar! Liar!*'
>
> And it sounded as if her voice was coming from everywhere, and the word echoed back from the great wall in the fog, muffled and changed, so that she seemed to be screaming Lyra's name, so that *Lyra* and *liar* were one and the same thing. (*The Amber Spyglass*, Scholastic, 2001, p. 308)

This time there is no angry denial; Lyra merely wilts into the arms of Will who shelters her and removes her from the immediate danger.

So in the Land of the Dead, Lyra is denounced and attacked for doing the very thing in which she excels and which has been so effective elsewhere: for telling tales. Shortly afterwards the strategy shifts. Lyra manages to harrow hell by *telling the truth*. When she encounters the ghosts who populate this barren land, Lyra regales them with true stories of her past packed with sensory detail. Her words are a rich source of sustenance to the ghosts and harpies who crowd around her. In the subsequent negotiations and bargain which is struck, it soon emerges that such accounts—grounded in truth and in personal observation—will assure the salvation of every single individual. A clear contrast is set up between this new system and that of the Church whose assertions about the afterlife are shown to be manipulative and misleading lies, nothing but empty threats and hollow promises.

From now on in the trilogy, true stories rather than tricks and inventions seem to be the order of the day. The dead who have so benefited from truth-telling instruct Mary Malone to follow suit, and it's in this way, by recounting a series of lived experiences, that she accomplishes the temptation and therefore guarantees redemption. What's more, Lyra herself is a seemingly reformed character. The

journey through the underworld clearly marks an important stage
in her development and maturation—emerging on the other side
both she and Will are "no-longer-quite-children" (p. 410). It also
seems to trigger a fundamental shift in her character. "I promise to
tell the truth, if you promise to believe it," she pledges in the trilogy's closing pages (p. 542). Pullman has elsewhere confirmed that
in the Land of the Dead: "She leaves fantasy behind, and becomes
a realist."[5]

The Great Betrayal?

Could *this* (rather than Roger's death or Pan's abandonment) be the
"great betrayal" prophesied for Lyra in the second chapter of the
trilogy? The treacherous act which the Master of Jordan College
knows she will commit unwittingly and at great emotional cost? In
telling the truth, is Lyra true to herself? Her conversion seems to go
against the very principles of realistic characterization upon which
Pullman sets such store: where, one might ask, is the plausibility,
the consistency? Nor is this betrayal limited to the character of Lyra
but extends to the trilogy overall and to its readers. It's as though
we, like Roger, are deftly led to a great precipice where the footing abruptly fails. The apparent 180-degree turn to the truth effectively pulls the rug out from under the reader who, for over a
thousand pages, has admired Lyra's ruses, enjoyed her fantastic
tales, and—crucially—relished the work of fantasy in which she
exists. Surely the implication is that we should all put away our
childish things and take up memoirs, autobiographies or confes-
sions instead? The move towards truth seems to fly in the face of
Pullman's own repeated valorization of stories and of storytellers,
those tricksters who (let's not forget) succeed in persuading someone of "something that isn't true." Is Pullman's hard-sell of truth his
ultimate act of treachery?

But should we believe him anyway when he—a storyteller—
states that storytellers deal in lies? Can you ever trust a (self-
avowed) trickster? How can we verify the truthfulness of his
statements? We are faced here with a literary equivalent of a classic, age-old philosophical conundrum commonly known as "The
Liar Paradox." Its earliest and most widely known formulation runs

---

[5] Philip Pullman, "Writing Fantasy Realistically," www.sofn.org.uk/conferences/
pullman2002.html, accessed 15th January, 2009.

as follows: "'The Cretans are always liars,' said the Cretan." Is the Cretan lying? If he is, his statement is true . . . which means that he is lying. Our mental footing starts to falter at this point. Lyra actually makes this kind of statement at one point in the trilogy: "You think I don't know about lying and that? I'm the best liar there ever was. But I en't lying to you, and I never will, I swear it" (*The Subtle Knife*, p. 107). Statements such as these appear irresolvable, impossible, and as disorientating as the trilogy's apparent move to truth. But just as philosophers have found ways around, and solutions to, the Liar Paradox so too is it possible to account for and understand the trilogy's own apparent paradoxes.

Solving the Paradox—"I En't dishonest"

Firstly, Lyra's character is by no means as clear-cut as Pullman suggests in his comments concerning her evolution. Even before the pivotal moment of the journey to the Land of the Dead (or *katabasis* as it was known to the Ancient Greeks), Lyra is more than capable of telling the truth. She's even been described by one critic as the "handmaiden of truth," no less.[6] In the trilogy's first chapter, she resists the temptation to run away or bury her head in the sand, and tells her "Uncle" the truth about the poisoned wine. In the course of the novel, she opens herself entirely to the Gyptians and, later, her father, recounting what has happened to her up until that particular point in the narrative. Similarly, in the second volume, and despite the considerable risks of incomprehension and rebuff, she perseveres in her efforts to truthfully explain herself and her experiences to both Mary and to Will. So what happens in the Land of the Dead *is* prepared for, it doesn't just come out of the blue. Lyra *has* done this before. Finally, of course, and long before her katabatic travels, Lyra is able to read the alethiometer. So the truth is literally at her fingertips.

Lies (Continued)

And if the truth makes many an appearance prior to the *katabasis*, so too do lies and deceptions continue to occur afterwards. Indeed, at the end of the very chapter in which the salvationary dimension

---

[6] Email correspondence with Rachel Falconer, author of *The Crossover Novel: Contemporary Children's Fiction and Its Adult Readership* (Routledge, 2009).

of truth is made clear, a lie is told—a white lie, a lie which seeks to assuage and comfort, but a lie nonetheless. Lyra asks Will whether the end is in sight: "He couldn't tell. But they were so weak and sick that he said, 'Yes, it's nearly over, we've nearly done it. We'll be out soon'" (*The Amber Spyglass*, p. 338). Later on, Will and Mary will "decide on a story and stick to it" in order to nego- tiate the authorities and generally navigate their way, once back in their own world (p. 540). And long after the apparent shift to the truth, Mrs. Coulter stays absolutely true to form as the most invet- erate of liars. The scene with Metatron is made up of a dizzying series of lies proclaiming themselves over and over as truths. Lyra's mother is perhaps the slipperiest of all the trilogy's characters, and even at this late stage in the proceedings, the reader is still not entirely sure what she's up to. Only because of the way the episode parallels Lyra's manipulation of the power-hungry bear is it possi- ble to perceive Mrs Coulter's (noble) treachery here.

Lies and Truth/Truth and Lies

But perhaps what really matters in all this is Lyra. Even the newly honest Lyra is not wholly exempt from breaking her word in the later stages of the trilogy. Lyra promises Mary that she and Will "won't go in among the trees" but, just six pages later, where else do we see them venturing but "into a little wood of silver-barked trees"?! (pp. 481, 489). It's also important to remember that it's towards the end of the trilogy that Lyra loses the ability to instinc- tively read the alethiometer. This means that there is a very clear overall balance within the overall work. Pre-*katabasis* she deliber- ately lies a great deal (although can tell the truth at times) and she can read the alethiomenter. Post-*katabasis* she endeavors to tell the truth (though does not manage it all the time) and—precisely because of that endeavor, that effort, and self-consciousness—is unable to read the truth-telling device. In short, truth and lies are distributed in a way which contributes to, rather than detracting from, the trilogy's internal coherence.

The cause of Lyra's loss will also be its cure: she will eventually regain her ability to reread the alethiometer by hard work and endeavor. Indeed, she will achieve something greater than her ini- tial gift, as the angel Xaphania informs her: "But your reading will be even better then, after a lifetime of thought and effort, because it will come from conscious understanding. Grace attained like that is deeper and fuller than grace that comes freely, and furthermore, once you've gained it, it will never leave you" (p. 520). The at first crippling but ultimately empowering consequences of self-consciousness are at the heart of Heinrich von Kleist's essay *On Marionette Theater* which Pullman cites in the Acknowledgements as one of his three main sources in the trilogy.

True Values: Choose Life

Another way out of the paradoxical impasse is in recognizing that the valorization of truth in the *katabasis* is by no means as out of kilter with the rest of the work as it may at first seem. We've seen with Will's words to Lyra in the Land of the Dead, or Mrs. Coulter's encounter with the Regent, that lies can be good, kind, and best while the truth can be deployed as a weapon intended to harm, manipulate, and annihilate. This is what Pullman is getting at when he chooses Blake's lines as the epigraph to Chapter 11 of *The Amber Spyglass*: "A truth that's told with bad intent beats all the lies you can invent." Truth is not, then, promoted—in the *katabasis* or elsewhere—for its own sake; it is not shown to be intrinsically valuable or good. It is instead a token or guarantee of something else: namely, a full life and an observant, appreciate liver of that life. "If they live in the world, they *should* see and touch and hear and love and learn things," says the harpy, and one senses Pullman close behind her (p. 334). Similarly, the ultimate crime of the Church is not the telling of lies as such but the life-arresting consequences of those lies. The destruction of "the joys and truthfulness of life" is poignantly embodied in the martyr encountered in the Land of the Dead who explains how the promise of heaven led to squander and desolation: "that's what led some of us to give our lives, and others to spend years in solitary prayer, while all the joy of life was going to waste around us, and we never knew" (*The Subtle Knife*, p. 283; *The Amber Spyglass*, p. 336). What's truly vaunted in this passage and in the trilogy overall is not truth *per se* but experience, gusto, joie de vivre. *Carpe diem*, remember well, and pass it on.

The Customer Comes First

Finally, we have to bear in mind the circumstances in which stories based on lived experiences and detailed personal observation come to the fore. We need to think about the communicative situation in which Lyra finds herself, and consider not only her motivation as speaker, but also the very particular requirements, needs and desires of her interlocutors (the dead). What's going on here is best understood by comparing this particular situation with one just prior to the entry into the land of the dead. The travelers spend the night before they set out in a shack in the suburbs of the dead. Their hosts are still alive, waiting for their deaths to come and lead them onwards. For this audience Lyra offers a narrative (a more elaborate version of which will soon be brutally rejected by the harpy) interweaving lived experience with invention. It's an action-packed tale of high adventure which is utterly condemned and dismissed by the narrator who refers to it scathingly as "this nonsense."[7] But her interlocutors respond very differently, gazing at her enthralled. For those who have been reduced to an existence of waiting, entirely devoid of action and events, Lyra's story is precisely what they require. Lyra's lies take them away from the misery of their present circumstances without any of the debilitating consequences of the Church's inventions.

The self-same story addressed to those cut off from the world and gorged on a surfeit of evil is, on the other hand, woefully inadequate. Lyra here totally misjudges the needs and interests of her listeners. She will not make the same mistake again. Her brief is so much clearer when she meets the ghosts who tell her directly what it is they want to hear: "the things they remembered, the sun and the wind and the sky, and the things they'd forgotten, such as how to play" (p. 328). In telling the ghosts "about the world," Lyra takes them back to their previous real, full existences and transports them from the land of the dead to the land of the living (p. 329). So if we compare these two moments, it becomes clear that truth satisfies the same escapist desires in the Land of the Dead as does fantasy in the land of the living. The promotion of truth at this particular moment in the story in no way implies a concurrent condemnation or disavowal of storytelling. Truth emerges instead as just one of the methods at the disposal of storytellers in order to move, to transport their listeners.

What is paramount, then, is the audience. Although it may seem that Pullman manipulates, misleads, and abuses his posi-

---

[7] *The Amber Spyglass*, p. 277. Writer and narrator rub shoulders here, since in "Writing Fantasy Realistically," Pullman speaks of "one of her Lyra-like fantasies, full of wild nonsense."

tion of trust, the overall thrust of the story is actually quite the reverse. If the trilogy has received the critical acclaim and popular success which it has, it is surely precisely because Pullman, like Lyra, has understood the importance of thinking about, anticipating, and responding to, the very different needs of his very diverse audience.

6
The Many Phases of Lyra

MARGARET MACKEY

The three dictionaries on my shelf tell me that ontology is "the part of philosophy that deals with the nature of reality," "part of metaphysics relating to the nature of existence," or "the branch of metaphysics concerned with the essence of things." Philip Pullman is happy to take on responsibility for the nature of his reality: the heroine of *His Dark Materials* flaunts the ontological complexity of any fiction through her name and pedigree: Lyra the liar, the daughter of "As-real."

Fiction *creates* essence, and reality, and existence of its own. Pullman uses mere words to develop invented worlds and people, and readers envisage them in their mind's eye. But what happens when that fictional essence, initially created through imaginative verbal engagement, turns into more concrete and tangible forms?

In this chapter I will discuss the ontological complications of three imaginary beings, Lyra, Pantalaimon, and the alethiometer, as they move from intangible existence on the page to a more incarnate life, embodied in a variety of ways from audio format to stage to screen to collectible doll.

In the novel of *The Golden Compass* (originally *Northern Lights*), Lyra and Pantalaimon, like many other characters in our written literature, first appeared in the form of abstract black marks on the page. Their only realization and animation took place in the minds of readers. Yet as the story moved into the mainstream of multimodal reworking (websites, audio performance, stage play, movie, videogame, dolls, and collectibles) Lyra and Pantalaimon became embodied in various ways, accessible to the eye, to the ear, and even to the hand. How does this transformation affect their imaginative reality?

Readers have plenty of practice in imagining the likes of the girl, Lyra. The readerly art of bringing characters to life in the mind has been developed over centuries. The dæmon, Pantalaimon, takes more imaginative effort; he's a new kind of being, part of Lyra but separate from her, able to disagree with her or to comfort her as need be. Readers must be able to comprehend *what* he is as well as the more familiar exercise of figuring out *who* he is. It is clear he is important; he appears in the fourth word of the book and so readers need to start comprehending his nature right from the beginning.

Understanding the nature of the dæmon is one of the intriguing elements of the early part of this story; experienced readers know that the authority for the existence of Lyra and Pan lies in the words of the author, and that it is both their duty and their pleasure as readers to comprehend and enliven the creatures established by the printed word. Understanding the dæmon was crucial to Pullman as well:

> The best idea I had was that it's only children's dæmons that change forms, and then [as the child gets older] they settle down. That's the real theme of the story: the difference between innocence and experience, in William Blake's terms.[1]

For readers, Pan is our first hint that the universe of *The Golden Compass* is not exactly the same as the one we live in, and as readers we know we must use the information of the book to develop an understanding that is not straightforwardly based on our own experiences of our own society. As readers we are thus prepared to accept that an alethiometer can have magical insight to the truth of present and future. Readers are schooled by experience to know that an invention presented in a book can be entirely imaginary. They do not expect or need to find support for the existence of the alethiometer in real life; the alethiometer belongs exclusively inside the pages. We may be able to bring a dæmon to imaginative life by considering its essence to be a metaphor for some important com-

---

[1] Quoted in Diane Roback, "Philip Pullman Confronts his Dæmons in New York," *Publishers Weekly* (1st November, 2007), www.publishersweekly.com/article/CA6496518.html, accessed November 4th, 2008.

ponents of being human in the world we actually inhabit. An alethiometer, on the other hand, is not a character with qualities we can extrapolate from our own human experience. It's simply a thing; the author presents it and we may accept its important role in the plot without giving it a great deal of further thought.

Yet it wasn't long after the publication of *The Golden Compass* that a different kind of affirmation of the alethiometer's existence and powers appeared, a support structure developed beyond the covers of the book.

Outside Support

The Golden Compass was published in 1995, and Random House, its American publishers, supported it with a website that, for the era, was lavish and imaginative. To this day, that website provides detailed background information about the alethiometer: a history of how it came to be, instructions on how to read it, and a detailed list of the symbols and some of their meanings. Readers exploring this site learn something about reading the alethiometer, but they are also likely to learn about reading the voice of Philip Pullman. Here, for instance, is part of the instructions for interpretation:

> The inquirer moves each of the hands in turn until it points to one of the three symbols.
>
> But that's only the physical part of the process. The other part is mental. The inquirer must endeavor to hold in his or her mind a clear picture of where each of the meanings comes in its range. Evoking the image of ladders with rungs extending downward is sometimes advised by skilled practitioners of alethiometry. Picture three ladders side by side, each rung being one meaning in the range, and mark distinctly the rungs corresponding to the meanings you intend—for example, by imagining a bright light shining on them, or ribbons tied around them, or by covering them in gold leaf. The inquirer must hold that image firmly, without losing it for a moment, while setting the hands in position.[2]

As a reader of *The Golden Compass*, I have learned to trust the lively and specific details that Pullman uses to make his fictional

---

[2] www.randomhouse.com/features/pullman/materials/materials.html, accessed September 14th, 2008.

world more credible. So when I recognize that tone, particularly in the suggestion to mark the rung of an imaginary ladder by covering it in gold leaf, I acknowledge that I am most plausibly dealing with the authority of the man who created the story in the first place. More than the imprimatur of the publisher's name on the website, this distinctive voice persuades me that this add-on to Lyra's world is authentic; my instinct for assessing the limits of fictional creation is satisfied. Yet the fictional veracity of these extra details is not confirmed in the traditional way by being presented within the covers of the book.

In an era of proliferating text forms, it may very well be that the period in which the book serves as its own self-sufficient authority is beginning to fade. As I write, Scholastic is advertising a new series for children, which tells the story by means of books, collectors' cards, and a videogame presented on a website.[3] Another recent example is *Cathy's Book*[4]: the book is described on Wikipedia as an Alternate Reality Game book, a fiction overlaid on the real world.[5] The hardback comes complete with an envelope of artifacts and the printed words of the story are overlaid with Cathy's doodles and larded with phone numbers and websites that really connect in our own world. Cathy even has her own entry on Facebook.[6]

The idea of a single narrative being distributed across several sites is becoming more commonplace, and we may expect more and more to see authoritative elements of the story appearing in complementary formats. These supporting fictions act somewhat like a flying buttress of a cathedral, a support that sustains a wall without being built directly in contact with it. The Pullman website was an early fore-runner of this kind of augmentation, and it raises interesting questions about whether readers respond with more conviction to this kind of *reinforced fiction* with all its supportive verisimilitude. Does a story feel more *real* when readers can locate evidence for its existence outside the covers of the book? Is it a gimmick or a deep change in how we understand narrative?

---

[3] Motoko Rich, "Author of Book Series Sends Kids on a Web Treasure Hunt," *New York Times* (1st September, 2008), www.nytimes.com/2008/09/02/books/02rior.html?fta=y, accessed September 14th, 2008; see also www.the39clues.com/, accessed September 14th, 2008.

[4] By Sean Stewart, Jordan Weisman, and Cathy Brigg (Running Press, 2006).

[5] http://en.wikipedia.org/wiki/Cathy's_book, accessed September 14th, 2008.

[6] http://www.new.facebook.com/people/Cathy_Vickers/1215800222, accessed September 14th, 2008.

As a child, I played with paper dolls. Some were mounted on a cardboard base and came with a second insert of cardboard to stand at right angles to the first, thus enabling the doll to stand independently. I am reminded of this effect when I see external sites of supporting fictional information. Do they play a similar effect, allowing the story to seem more "free-standing" and "real"? In the end, it's all still just cardboard, all still a made-up effect. Yet the creation of a stronger feeling of verisimilitude is undeniable.

Gaining a Voice

In 1999, Listening Library in association with Random House released an unabridged audio version of *The Golden Compass*.[7] Narrated by Pullman himself and enacted by a large cast of characters, it presents nearly eleven hours of narrative. Now Lyra (Joanna Wyatt) and Pantalaimon (Rupert Degas) are given voices. The characters remain invented, but the real voices create measurable and recordable sound waves. They reflect gender, they speak with particular accents and cadences, they provide a fixed pacing for the processing of the words. In these specific and in other less tangible ways, they develop and present character and atmosphere.

In some ways a dramatic reading of a narrative text provides the most interesting interface between written fiction and what we commonly consider the real world. Normally an unabridged audio recording is the only adaptation of a printed work that keeps all or nearly all of the words (a dramatic version may drop such expressions as "said Lyra"). And yet the abstract of the verbal fiction is rendered concrete in particular, limited ways; we are skilled at interpreting the means by which a specific voice represents character and personality (and in the case of this Lyra in this recording, represents class as well; Lyra does not speak with the received English of her guardians but with the demotic accent of the Oxford streets). Lyra's physical appearance remains abstract in the audio recording, but she is no longer a figment purely of the mind; she has physical properties, even if they are considerably restricted. Likewise, we have a specific sense of Pantalaimon; even if we managed to read the book vaguely perceiving Pan only as a kind of

---

[7] *The Golden Compass*. Unabridged audiobook. Listening Library/Random House, 1999.

abstract and nebulous, shape-shifting appendage to Lyra, we must now acknowledge his separate voice, different gender, and apparent physical reality. Even as he changes form, his voice remains constant, and this constancy becomes a psychological "fact" about Pan that we are probably hard-wired to take into account.

Managing the Dæmons

In 2003, Nicholas Hytner oversaw the adaptation of the three books of *His Dark Materials* into a stage play that was presented at the National Theatre in London.[8] The massive story was communicated in two three-hour plays, performed at a brisk pace on a revolving stage; one scene faded into another at high speed.

For the stage play, the dæmons had to become not merely voiced but also embodied. Pan's shape-shifting talents, so simple to describe and imagine in print, so invisible and untroubling in audio, provide a major imaginative challenge for the director and the audience when they have to be incarnated in some way on the stage. Hytner's response was inspired. On stage, Pantalaimon and other dæmons were presented in puppet form. The puppeteer, clad in black with face hidden by a black balaclava, provided movement and voice, and stage-managed the shift between one hand-puppet form and another. Smaller dæmons could be carried by the actors.

The development of the stage dæmons emerged and evolved in complex ways through the imaginative co-operation of many people. Robert Butler describes some of the artifice involved:

> The puppet department was working with the actors, the directors and the costume-makers, to find ways of placing the dæmons on the bodies, ways of making slits and gaps in the costumes to conceal part of the dæmons, ways of attaching magnets and mounts to the costumes to hold the dæmons, and ways of threading fine string from the puppets through the costumes and onto a ring on the hand of an actor, so that he could twitch the beak or flutter the wings of his dæmon bird. The nature of the dæmons was changing too: sometimes it was only necessary to create the head and the tail, as the body could be concealed within the clothing.[9]

---

[8] Adapted by Nicholas Wright. *Philip Pullman's His Dark Materials* (Nick Hern Books, 2003).

[9] Robert Butler, *The Art of Darkness: Staging the Philip Pullman Trilogy* (National Theatre/Oberon Books, 2003), p. 78.

Although in any concrete analysis of the presences on the stage, the puppeteer was a real person and the puppets who collectively represented the singular character of Pantalaimon were toys, audiences were able to make the imaginative transition to "read" life from the puppet's movements and fade the puppeteer more or less out of consciously observed existence. The success of this theatrical sleight of hand reaches its culmination in a moment in the second play when Lyra must speak to the figure of her own death; Pan's puppeteer pulls off his balaclava and speaks as Lyra's death. The effect is electrical; the puppeteer has been effectively invisible for many hours by this point, and to find he has a role *inside* the world of the story is a huge surprise.

The power of the audience's theatrical imagination is strong enough to overwhelm specific incarnated information about the actual bodies on the stage. The puppeteer holds the Pan puppet and his arm makes it move; the voice comes from the actor not from the toy. Yet audiences appear to find it relatively effortless to ascribe all the elements of life to the puppet in terms of engaging with the story being enacted on the stage. The ontology of the make-believe is triumphant—and the ontology of the make-believe, after the shock of the puppeteer's invasion of the story world at the point where Lyra meets her death, takes over once again, and audiences once more "read" the puppet as Pan. The capacity of that virtual existence to outweigh the corporeal realities on the stage is a remarkable testimonial to the flexibility of human minds and human powers of observation.

The program for the stage play provided some interesting "flying-buttress" support both for the dæmons and for the alethiometer. "Philip Pullman considers," says the program, "that previously unrecognized dæmons have appeared in portraits throughout the ages. Some are shown, here and on following pages."[10] The program is decorated with famous "real" portraits and woodcuts of individuals accompanied by animals, creating virtual "evidence" to support the existence of dæmons through history. An insert in the centre of the program includes instructions on how to read the alethiometer, using much the same wording as the website. In this context, however, the ring of Pullman's authorial voice resonates differently, since the text being supplemented is the playscript, not the novel.

---

[10] *His Dark Materials*, play program, 2003.

The elaborated world of the stage play thus draws on many kinds of support for the imaginative construction of the fictional world. But the real-life bodies required to appear on the stage, in ways designed to attract attention in some cases and to deflect it in others, made their own demands on the production. Many of these requirements could simply be edited out of the way in the film version.

Enter the Computer Graphic

In creating a movie, the makers of *The Golden Compass* had many more ingredients with which to compose the ever-changing figure of Pantalaimon. Computer-graphics animation allowed the play of dæmon shape-shifting to be an element of the film's visual pleasures.

The film-makers, however, seem to have been uneasy about the capacity of audiences to figure out the role of the dæmon as the story advanced. Alone among all the adaptations, they begin the whole story with a definition of what a dæmon is and does. A voice-over on the opening shot says, "There are many universes and many earths parallel to each other. Worlds like yours where people's souls live inside their bodies—and worlds like mine where they walk beside us as animal spirits we call dæmons."[11] The first words of dialogue in the movie are spoken by the dæmon Stelmaria to Lord Asriel.

DVDs, with their excess of memory, have made us accustomed to the extra scenes of "how we made this movie." Adhering to this convention, the DVD release of the 2007 movie gives us a great deal of background information about the creation of the dæmons. Interestingly, the producers do not just focus exclusively on the clever animatronics, but also give us a sense of Pullman creating the dæmon out of ink and paper in the first place. We see his hands typing on a computer keyboard; he tells us how he wrote draft after draft of the first chapter and got nowhere until the day when he picked up his pen and found himself writing "Lyra and her dæmon" without any real idea of what it meant.

Pullman provides added insight into the ontological proprieties of being a fictional dæmon in print form: "The reason the dæmon

---

[11] *The Golden Compass*. Chris Weitz, Director. DVD. Montreal: Alliance Films/ New Line Home Entertainment, 2008/2007.

works on the page when we read the book is that I only draw your attention to it when the dæmon needs to do something or say something. Otherwise we can forget it's there and it doesn't clutter up the place, doesn't get in the way."

The more corporeal the dæmon, the greater its talent for adding "clutter" to an imagined world. There are some readers whose mind's eye maintains every detail of the mental image they have created; many others "tidy away" any component of the story that is not in active engagement in the moment. The imaginative focus of such readers often works in close-up, as the mind acts as operator of the "camera" that brings characters and settings to life in the mind. To such forgetful readers, only what's in close focus actually exists as a centre for attention; the rest fades to a kind of mental half-life away from the spotlight of the imagination. But a fleshed-out dæmon, on stage or screen, cannot so easily fade from view, and persists in occupying our line of sight. It is one form of contrast between the imagined fictions of readers and those of viewers, one that has received little critical attention.

Distributed Dæmons

The official website for the movie offers users the chance to establish what their own dæmon would be. You provide your name, check male or female, and answer twenty questions about yourself on a sliding scale, and you are supplied with a named animal that you may request to have sent to your email address or embedded in your blog or MySpace site.[12]

If this dæmon in this way becomes part of your own virtual identity, does that change its ontological status? Does it change yours? If we people our own world with virtual dæmons, ascribe a particular dæmon to ourselves, what are the consequences for how we perceive ourselves? There are precedents for acquiring the labels of an externalized virtual identity; I can describe myself, for example, as a Scorpio from the zodiac, or as a Rat from the Chinese calendar; why not be a person whose dæmon is Archeleron, the Crow? (One possible answer is that my identity as Scorpio and Rat is persistent, whereas if I forget to answer the twenty questions consistently, I get a new dæmon identity every time. Perhaps

---

[12] www.goldencompassmovie.com/?undefined, accessed September 28, 2008.

another answer lies in the commercial framing of the dæmon iden-
tification website—which is not to say that astrology is devoid of
money-making interests.)

For most people, the acquisition of a dæmon from this website
will simply entail another form of playful engagement with the fictional world, and the status of the dæmon will be qualified by its
link to that specific fiction, rather than taking on a firmer identity
and role in someone's life more generally.

Playing the Game

Inevitably, as part of the blockbuster promotion of the filmed version of *The Golden Compass*, a videogame[13] was marketed at the
same time. In the game, Pantalaimon retains his essential quality of
shape-shifting but the ontological status of this quality represents a
radical change. Pan's multiple options are reduced to four, and,
more importantly, he now changes shape at the behest of the
player as part of the pursuit of the game's goals. The *Official Guide*
to the game explains how this works:

> At Lyra's request [expressed when the player clicks the mouse], Pan
> can transform into whichever creature suits her needs.
>   If she needs a keen eye, Pan can take his ermine form. If Lyra
> needs to cross a wide gap, the wings of Pan's hawk are just the thing.
> Similarly, Pan can swing Lyra across large gaps by transforming into a
> sloth with long nimble arms. Pan's wildcat form allows Lyra to climb
> certain surfaces like nets and fabric.[14]

Some (but only some) of Pan's shifts in the book are similarly pur-
posive. In the game all extraneous, miscellaneous, or playful movement is sacrificed to a strict utilitarianism. The player gains a limited
power over the mystique of shape-shifting but only for very restric-
tive ends.

I spoke once to a young man who was a heavy gamer and also
a voracious reader. He spoke eloquently of the difference between
the two formats. On balance, he found reading more immersive
and engaging, but there were times, he said, when a reader, faced

---

[13] *The Golden Compass.* Sony PSP game. Sega, 2007.

[14] Fernando Bueno, *The Golden Compass: Prima Official Game Guide* (Prima
Games, 2007), p. 6.

with the inability to change a syllable of the story, feels quite "futile." Readers and viewers have probably always taken mental liberties with the stories they read and watch. But many contemporary readers and viewers have access to alternative ways of experiencing fictions interactively, with some of the agency of a character transferred to the player. In this case, that agency is limited, but it still represents a change in the force animating the character of Pantalaimon. Readers who have even this limited control over the story in their game-playing may be more likely to notice the absence of such control in their reading and viewing. Submission to the story being told is no longer the normal, unnoticed stance that we once took completely for granted. Exposure to alternative ways of engaging with a fiction enable us to articulate what was once normal and invisible: a reader's powerlessness in the face of print's authority and fixity. A dæmon we can change ourselves is a different kind of being from a dæmon who changes at the will of the author.

The Dæmon Doll

The Tonner Doll company produces high-quality collectible dolls, many of them based on film characters. In 2008, their *Golden Compass* collection offers ten different dolls, based on the characters of Lyra, Mrs. Coulter, Lord Asriel, and Lee Scoresby. The materiality of the dolls (and even more so, the scrupulously detailed materiality of their clothes) is stressed in the online catalogue. The following quote describes one of the two Lyra dolls, the one that comes complete with dæmon and alethiometer:

> The clever little liar comes with the mystical "alethiometer" and wears a high-detailed costume. Lyra wears a knit undershirt paired with a cotton skirt [*sic*.] with "aurora borealis" inspired printing and printed cotton skirt. In addition, she wears magenta knit tights, cozy faux fur boots, warm knit mittens, multi-colored crocheted cap, and an opulent embroidered jacket with shaggy trimmed hem, embroidered trim, and wooden beads; Pantalaimon (Pan) ferret dæmon and display stand included.[15]

This doll offers a tangible, highly specified version of Lyra, an alethiometer you can hold in your hand, and a singular incarnation

---

[15] www.tonnerdoll.com/gcompass.htm, accessed October 12th, 2008.

of Pan (not furry, as might be expected, but made out of some hard material such as resin and bearing a trademark statement on his underbelly). The status of this dæmon doll is intriguing. Here is a dæmon you could actually carry about in your own pocket— except for the taboo that strictly outlaws touching anybody else's dæmon. Can you touch this doll of Pan if you are pretending to be Lyra and activating the Lyra doll by means of your own imagination? Or to play authentically, should you always use the Lyra doll's hands to touch the Pan doll? Perhaps the power of trespass is part of the appeal of playing with dolls in the first place, in which case you can over-ride the rules of the story with impunity or with glee.

Do such scruples matter at all in the world of collectibles, or is the capacity to hold the fictional character in your own hands and "play by your own rules" the over-arching purpose of acquiring a collectible to begin with? How does the tactile existence of the dolls intersect or overlap with their imaginative reality? As more and more collectible dolls are based on fictional texts already in existence, these questions become more intriguing.

The One in the Many

What is striking about this collection of versions of a single story is its commonplace qualities. Many popular stories are told over and over again, in different formats and using different vehicles. Young people today grow up in a world in which they take it for granted that their fictional constructs will manifest an ever-broadening range of ontological variability, and that being embodied in many different media can often be seen as part of the essence of being a fiction. Readers (and listeners and viewers and players and doll-owners) will respond diversely to this range of Lyras and Pantalaimons. Some will mentally compose an *ur*-Lyra that encompasses and over-rides every version they meet. Others will react selectively, accepting some versions and rejecting others for reasons they may or may not be able to articulate.

What consistent qualities make Lyra Lyra? What imaginative resources do we draw on in order to recognize her whether she is voiced by Joanna Wyatt (in the audio version) or represented both visually and aurally by Anna Maxwell Martin or Elaine Symons (in the stage play) or by Dakota Blue Richards (in the film)—or by the doll modeled on the features of Richards? What is the essence that causes us to remember these different actresses as "Lyra" rather than as their several selves? Is it as simple as their participation in a plot we recognize as the story of *The Golden Compass*? That basic premise would be more persuasive were it not for the well-known phenomenon that makes viewers reject some actors as "wrong", no matter how familiar the events of the plot.

As for Pantalaimon, he is less bound by the specificities of a human actor, and can be created in puppet or computer-animated form. What essential imaginative fuel must viewers add in order to appreciate him as a fully-alive phenomenon?

Stories in the Mind

In 1908, E.B. Huey said that to understand what we do when we read would represent "the acme of a psychologist's achievements, for it would be to describe very many of the most intricate workings of the human mind, as well as to unravel the tangled story of the most remarkable specific performance that civilization has learned in all its history."[16] Part of this remarkable and mysterious achievement of reading is the creation in the mind of ontologically satisfying fictional characters out of a cognitive and imaginative mix that Victor Nell once described as "all air and thought."[17] In this chapter I have simply outlined something of the scale of the questions that demand to be answered. As we move through numerous complexly-elaborated fictional worlds, we take much for granted about how we understand essence, reality, and existence in universes that, tangible or not, come to life only in terms of make-believe.

Does Asriel's daughter become more "real" as she is voiced and given physical movement, embodied in the live flesh of actresses or in the doll's imitation body? Does she establish her fictional "reality" regardless of medium, or indeed *in spite of* the qualities of those who represent plural incarnations of her singular personality? When we understand the ontological grounding of fiction, we will certainly be a giant step closer to understanding the intricacies of the human mind.

---

[16] E.B. Huey, *The Psychology and Pedagogy of Reading* (MIT Press, 1968/1908), p. 6.

[17] Victor Nell, *Lost in a Book: The Psychology of Reading for Pleasure* (Yale University Press, 1988), p. 1.

7

Kicking Up Some Dust

MARY HARRIS RUSSELL

> . . . there are some interesting things going on down there in the realm of the very small.
>
> —PHILIP PULLMAN, "The Elementary Particles of Narrative"

Humans need stories as a way of understanding the world. According to Santiago Colas, the stories in *His Dark Materials* "serve as creative indicators of a portion of reality: with them in mind, their listeners may rearrange their relationship to themselves and to the world around them in a more congenial fashion."[1] Colas explains that stories imagine "a certain relationship between matter and spirit, body and mind." In that relationship, Dust is born. Stories, long and short, generate Dust.

Pullman tells his stories, in forms long and short, appearing over a period of years and raising constant questions as to our processing of a multi-volume text. *His Dark Materials*, once considered a completed trilogy, has been amplified in several directions, both on stage at London's National Theatre in 2003 and in print, in two small volumes, *Lyra's Oxford* in 2003 and *Once Upon a Time In The North* in 2008.

In each of these post-*Amber Spyglass* stories, the characters' histories are moved into either a sequel or a prequel, and both appear in print with additional pieces of apparently real ephemera—maps, brochures, postcards, memos and even a game—mixed in with the

---

[1] "Telling True Stories, or The Immanent Ethics of Material Spirit (and Spiritual Matter) in Philip Pullman's *His Dark Materials*," *Discourse: Journal for Theoretical Studies in Media and Culture* 27:1 (Winter 2005), p. 11.

story or gathered at the end. Pullman is now at work on something he characterizes as an even earlier prequel, *The Book of Dust.*

If we look at some important story-telling moments both in the trilogy and in Pullman's later and most playful pieces, we can see that the self emerging through the processes of story telling is not only Lyra's and Lee's but the reader's as well. The process which generates truth becomes the most important aspect of Pullman's revisions of familiar stories—whether religious myths, school stories, or westerns. When the author sends the story off in a direct direction, the resultant tale is about something much larger than a deity and a garden, or an atlas, or a history book. Truth comes from the process of constructing it, and it is in the context of relations between human and events that Dust regenerates itself. As Colas concludes, "the self in Pullman's universe is relational and becoming (rather than being.)" We become the stories we tell and the stories we read.

Dust for the First Time, Dust for the Meantime

Critics have often noted Lyra's progression as a storyteller in the trilogy, especially as she moves from simpler to more complicated conceptions of truth.[2] Late in *The Golden Compass*, Lord Asriel, trying to explain Dust to Lyra, reads aloud from an Adam and Eve narrative that is Genesis re-written to include dæmon-settling. Lyra is astounded that he's using the story as a piece of evidence. Hadn't the Cassington Scholar at Jordan told her "it was just a kind of fairy tale"? Her father counters with a defense of stories:

> But think of Adam and Eve like an imaginary number, like the square root of minus one; you can never see any concrete proof that it exists, but if you include it in your equations, you can calculate all manner of things that couldn't be imagined without it.

Throughout the volumes of the trilogy, Lyra is learning how to use stories that are fantasy or deception to save herself and her cause.

[2] See Naomi Wood's "Paradise Lost and Found: Obedience, Disobedience, and Storytelling in C.S. Lewis and Philip Pullman," *Children's Literature in Education* 32:4 (December 2001), pp. 237–259; Mary Harris Russell, "Ethical Plots, Ethical Endings in Philip Pullman's *His Dark Materials*," in *Foundations* 33 (Summer 2003), pp. 68–75.

She "had to be vague in some places and invent plausible details in others; she had to be an artist, in short." Her development, however, changes direction in the land of the Dead when Lyra finally realizes that only "true" stories will liberate the souls from their gray afterlife.

Less attention has been paid to Mary Malone's role as storyteller in *His Dark Materials*. Early on, she is fatigued and disappointed. Her research scoffed at, her lab scheduled for closing and her funding dried up, she needs a story in which she can believe, and she needs the confirming belief of others. Lyra arrives to give these, but she does so by enabling Malone to turn her scientific ways of knowing into tools rather than destinations. When Malone decides to follow Lyra—and hence to see if Dark Matter and Dust are real—she can only do so, initially, by telling a lie to the guard at the hornbeam tree opening. Grown-up as she is, she must "tell a story" as children do, to join the larger process of creating Lyra's story and what we eventually come to see as the larger process of keeping Dust alive in the universes.

In *The Amber Spyglass*, where Malone plays her largest role, she uses her scientific story-telling tools—working through the particulars, examining why the seed-pod trees of the mulefa are dying, and gauging the ecological effects of that for all worlds. Atal, a mulefa, tells her story to Mary (another Genesis variation) because, as Atal says, "humans can see connections and possibilities and alternatives that are invisible to us." Mary uses her scientific construction skills to make a spyglass out of amber, a tool that will enable her to see the Dust involved. What Malone then can see, in fact, is the story, or the possible stories.

Malone fulfills one additional role in this volume and this is as a storyteller for Will and Lyra, conveying not only scientific but emotional knowledge to them. Like Raphael in Milton's *Paradise Lost*, the "sociable spirit" (Book 5, 221), who is sent to spend the day with Adam and Eve, "as friend with friend" (229), Mary must put into place one remaining piece of Lyra's and Will's adult identities. It is through the telling of Malone's own story—of how she discovered passion and love and decided to step outside the rigidly defined world in which she lived as a nun—that she can bring Lyra and Will to the story of their adult lives and prepare them for the moment of free will. Malone's story is not one of a departure from celibacy that subsequently made everything magically wonderful.

That first lover was not, for her, the love to end all loves, nor was her life redefined as passion-centered or statically happy. The difference is adult. Malone tells of missing a sense of connectedness with the universe in her life after she has left the religious world. And it is only when she has seen the movement of the cloud of Dust that she has sensed once again the essential connectedness of the universe. To reach the perception that "Matter *loved* Dust," she must be engaged in a continuing process, in continuing dynamic connections with life, rather than having any one plot point in a life or story bestow value to that story or life.

There has been much discussion of just exactly what kind of an awakening takes place between Will and Lyra in the next days of the plot, but Pullman has chosen to leave it unspecified. For the purposes of my argument here, it is not important to establish what happened but rather to note that only after the awakening are Will and Lyra given significant details about the rest of their lives, as their dæmons convey to them that the "windows" leaking Dust must be closed and that those closures necessitate their parting forever. (Serafina Pekkala has conveyed the information to the dæmons, before their reunion with Will and Lyra.) Mary Malone would not be the appropriate messenger here, for she is external to them. The knowledge and the choice based on that knowledge must come from within them, must come, in fact from that externalized combination of spirit and soul which is each persona's dæmon.

For one more brief moment, the story-telling spotlights shifts back to Lyra at the end of the trilogy. Will and Mary Malone have agreed that they will share a common fiction about who they are in their Oxford, but it will be only strategically true. Speaking to Dame Hannah and the Master of Jordan College, in her own Oxford, Lyra seems to hold a rather certain concept of the relation between her story and the truth. "My true story's too important for me to tell you if you're only going to believe half of it. So I promise to tell the truth, if you promise to believe it." She laments her lost facility with the alethiometer but is told that she can relearn it, from books in Bodley's Library. Off to the library. End of story.

Not end of story. Pullman unsettles both Lyra's certainty and even the reader's certainties about other figures from the trilogy (Lee Scoresby and Iorek Byrnison), suggesting that the dynamic of process is more important than a settled arrival at certainties. The brevity of these next two texts—almost a parodic inversion of the lengthy trilogy—allow us to focus on smaller stories, with, perhaps, larger metaphoric implications about just how Dust needs to be preserved in the world. Both *Lyra's Oxford* and *Once Upon a Time in the North* have mostly flown under the critical radar, though for different reasons. *Lyra's Oxford* appeared three years after the trilogy was completed, and when most public fan attention was directed toward the upcoming movie. *Once Upon a Time in the North* will probably attract more attention, because it is longer and the movie has now appeared. Readers have seen an armored bear. Readers have seen Lyra and Lee Scoresby, embodied by Dakota Blue Richards and Sam Elliott.

Answers: Looking Up at the Sky

In *Lyra's Oxford*, the story is subtitled "Lyra and the Birds," and can be summarized briefly. Lyra and Pan observe the birds of Oxford seeming to attack another bird traveling through. That bird is actually a witch's dæmon—we remember that witches can travel far from their dæmons—coming to seek special medication from an obscure Oxford alchemist. Or so he says. Lyra and Pan must find the alchemist, but when they do, they discover that their initial appraisal of who's good and who's bad is far off course.

Within the covers, additional materials are presented, interleaved or at the end: an illustrated foldout map of Oxford—which can only be viewed by interrupting the reading process—complete with advertisements that allude to *His Dark Materials* (an advertisement for a book written by Marisa Coulter, or a guide to Svalbard). At the end, there is a picture postcard of Oxford, front and back, and a brochure of a cruise ship. A hand-written notation on the brochure references a meeting at a café. Does that describe the café in the world beyond the hornbeam trees? Or does it speak of something we haven't yet seen? Readers are tantalized with material out of which they want to make something. Readers and characters will struggle with this impulse.

The process of story telling and story-reading is central in several ways here. First, the plot in which Lyra and Pan are engaged shows that the literary form of a detective story—whether with Nancy Drew or Sherlock Holmes at the center—cannot explain reality so neatly. Initially, Lyra thinks she's read the clues about what's happening correctly, but she has not and discovers at the end that she has been, in fact, manipulated as a character in someone's else's story.

Second, the additional objects included within the covers hint at both what we know and what we cannot know. Lyra's journey and the reader's are proceeding in parallel tracks. Throughout this first bagatelle, we find a concern with how we know and how dependably we can know that carries on *His Dark Materials'* fascination with how humans know and why they tell stories. As "the author" of the preface tells readers:

> *This book contains a story and several other things. The other things might be connected with the story, or they might not; they might be connected to stories that haven't appeared yet. It is not easy to tell.*

Lyra's Oxford actually begins with two addresses directly to the reader—a frontispiece quotation describing Oxford (taken from an actual book), but attributed to one Oscar Baedecker's *The Coasts of Bohemia* and a preface from an author. It is not signed by Philip Pullman (nor by anyone else), but the reference to the coasts of Bohemia might make us feel entwined in a fictional world.

Early on, Lyra speaks "severely" to Pan when he suggests that the starlings overhead may mean nothing. "Everything means something . . . We just have to find out how to read it." Yet she herself is finally revealed as having rushed too fast to settle on a meaning. We follow her reliance upon such diverse sources as personal recollections, local legends, scholarly point of view, and street maps, all of which initially seem appealing because they might bring an end to uncertainty. Yet the map, for example, which bears a hand-written notation at the top, "Mary Malone lives here," is inserted literally into the text so that it breaks into a question about time, which would seem a certainty but is not necessarily so. Lyra wants certainty; Pan is urging her to slow down: "Don't. Wait. Hush." Lyra's own ego-involvement as the flawed puzzle-solver reminds us also that Lyra is now growing to maturity in the world of scholars, not of armored polar bears, where a tourist map also carries ads for esoteric scholarly books and nothing is quite as it seems.

Lyra's not the only one being encouraged to make mistakes in interpretations. Through his use of a variety of birds, all of which have established allusive or connotative backgrounds, Pullman leads the reader on to make something of it. The starlings are gritty, urban, unloved birds, and yet we learn eventually that they were acting to protect Lyra. The swan arrives, not like an isolated

Zeusian sexual antagonist, as we might have thought, but hurtles in like a protective bodyguard and one who must be returned to his community at the end. The nightingale song provides more solace than answers: we know now that Will's dæmon is a nightingale and that Will and his dæmon can function apart from each other, but could this nightingale be Kirjava? Both Lyra and the reader learn that the ability to stay open to meaning and process is more important than the ability to close down too fast on a conclusion. At the end, after Lyra and Pan have left the alchemist, Sebastian Makepeace, and they wonder about the sound of a bird,

> 'Things don't mean things as simply as that,' Lyra said, uncertainly. 'Do they?'

Lyra's last act is to put "the crumbs out on the windowsill, for the birds." She is affirming a nurturing connection with actual birds, as well as with birds as either objects of interpretation or actors in her story. Her journey has been one from certainty and answers to questions and uncertainty. The reader's has been parallel. Makepeace has refused to explain everything: "It means something about you, and something about the city. You'll find the meaning if you search for it. Now you better go."

Answers: Looking Down on the Earth

And so we go, the narrative-hungry fans of Pullman, looking for another crumb, until 2008 and the appearance of *Once Upon A Time in the North*. The book begins—still tiny but almost twice the size of *Lyra's Oxford*—with a breathless cascade of prose bringing us Lee Scoresby's balloon, making a less than graceful landing in the gritty seaport town of Novy Odense. This is not the scholarly world of Lyra's Oxford but an adventurous and entrepreneurial frontier town. In both, however, there are things to be figured out—who's good, who's bad, and what should be done. Scoresby sets down, almost penniless, sardonic, and laconic, as we have known him to be, in a frontier town with many problems. Why is a captain not being allowed to remove his cargo from the warehouse and leave the harbor? Why is the election for mayor of this undistinguished town such a hot contest? Why is there an experienced and nasty gunslinger in town? Who are all these bears loitering around? And, is there any hope for a small ray of true love, somewhere, is this dirty, smelly town? Both within the text and on the back end-papers we find a variety of other documents, or partial documents—a few pages from a manual on aeronautics, correspondence about Lyra's dissertation, a game called "Peril of the Pole."

Without providing spoilers about this mini-adventure in the Western genre, let me suggest some patterns visible here which tie Lee's story to Lyra's, as both bagatelles give us an exercise in keeping our narrative or interpretive options open. Both stories prepare us for the dynamisms of whatever story Pullman will now choose to unfold about Dust.

In *Once Upon a Time in the North*, Lee must learn to re-write, re-invent his own story. He must work out, as he does in initially leaving the balloon's gondola, "which way up he was." Though he tries to assume the "nonchalance proper to a prince of the air," Novy Odense sees only a balloon jockey with too little money and too many questions.

Lee must figure out Novy Odense, and Pullman emphasizes his senses—hearing, vision, and smell—in learning the territory. It looks, initially like "the bleakest, smelliest, most unfriendliest place we've ever set foot in." The prices for supplies are too high, the natives not friendly. Though his senses sometimes betray him, as when he's moved by the soft and sweet-smelling Olga, Stepford-daughter of the politician Poliakov, more often what he sees makes a crucial difference in the story. He "knows the look of men like that." People have a certain "look" and they are looked at. The captain's first words to him are "What are you looking at?" Iorek Byrnison makes his first appearance settling "watchfully" by the side of the harbor. He protects the drunken captain of the impounded cargo ship when the captain doesn't see what's happening but Lee does, when "the bartender raised his stick, and was about to bring it down when Lee moved."

Only later does he discover that he is protecting someone who's on the opposite side from the villainous Larsen Manganese thugs. He sees and notices the model of a giant tank-mounted, armored gun, just before the bad guys whisk it away. When a nasty gunfighter makes an appearance under an assumed name, Lee says, in recognizing him, "Then I got keener eyesight than you do." He hears the sounds of approaching trouble from footwear or claws or tank tracks. When trying to rescue the cargo from the warehouse, he uses his eyes, or Hester's, to construct and solve a living word problem: where are the remaining gunmen and who has how many shots left, to be delivered at what angle. He knows it's a bad situation because "there's no one in sight." He improvises to use the inner lid of a cigarillo tin to make a mirror.

Throughout much of the early investigation of Novy Odense, his dæmon, Hester, must try to keep him out of trouble, with remarks like, "Find a bed, Lee. Keep still. Don't talk to anyone. Think good thoughts. Stay out of trouble." Or, later, "If you don't watch your step, you'll be under it [the ground]." Hester grumbles from inside his coat when he is entranced by Poliakov's daughter, and after he has struggled to find the correct response to questions about matters of the heart from his fellow lodger, Victoria Lund, Hester tells him he was correct, but chides him for not realizing what was being discussed (a marriage proposal). And it's Hester's eyesight that is so crucial inside the warehouse.

Scoresby's vision and good heart can only take him so far. He is able to free the cargo, get it to the ship, and get the captain launched out of the harbor. It is Hester, however, who alerts him to the details of the final resolution, which comes from behind him—the menacing gun, which Iorek destroys, is followed by the Larsen Manganese soldiers. It is Lt. Haugland—the officer of the Customs and, now we find out, the intended fiancé of Victoria Lund—who knows what to do next, and it's Hester and Iorek who get Lee finally to the get-away boat and the get-away balloon. Haugland also explains what neither Lee nor Hester can actually see—the invisible subtext of the scene, Larsen Manganese's interest in the mineral-rich ore samples which can establish a claim.

The story actually ends with a wry remark by Hester, affirming that her inner vision is just as strong as her actual eyes. Iorek has just informed her that she is not, in fact, a mere jackrabbit from the nation of Texas, but an arctic hare: "Iorek's right. I always knew I had more class than a rabbit."

At the end, we find attached documents, which appear to be part of dissertation material by one Lyra Silvertongue. She's checking with her dissertation director on details, figuring out the proper form of documentation. She also includes a clipping of a news report of the incident we have just read and seen in our heads, authored by Oskar Sigurdsson, a journalist clearly on the side of the bad guys. The Lyra we glimpse here is becoming more accomplished at living in her actual, scholarly world and at going slowly through the processes of making meaning, in a context, for a purpose. Toward the end of *Lyra's Oxford*, Lyra thinks to herself, "Oh, how stupid she could be when she was being clever!" Later, apparently, she has learned to think and write strategically, to gain the goal of her dissertation being accepted—and we have that document—yet we have been clearly reminded that she knows so much more than her advisors about some of the characters involved. She has learned to hold and preserve diverse knowledges, diversely.

The final added document, a board game entitled "Peril of the Pole," presents more puzzles. After unfolding and assembling the game and reading the rules, we discover that it isn't really a race to the pole, but almost to the pole. Anyone who would reach the pole itself would be sucked down into the vortex of the earth. Yet the game is a game, a child's game, and reminds us of the way in which any game is a story, and any story a game, and the meaning of both games and stories must be in relationship to someone or something else.

Coming to Dusty Conclusions

Lyra makes an initial series of mistakes because she tries to treat the world as if it provides the certainty that some people think the alethiometer provides. (She herself does know that the alethiometer requires a ranging through various levels and delivers messages often metaphoric rather than literal.) Lee also sometimes forgets that the world's reality is more than the sum of its sensory parts and that life is sometimes more complicated than a geometric puzzle. Both approaches are successful to a point, but their limitations are indicated, as is the necessity of maintaining a dynamic relationship with one's dæmon. At the end of both books, puzzles remain. Makepeace, the alchemist, refuses a larger explanation, for the time being. We don't know all that Lee and Iorek are headed for, even though we are reminded of some of it, in the flash-forward to Lee cradling his Winchester at the time of his death.

Both stories are bagatelles but offered not only for our amusement but also as reminders of the central concerns that lie before us in the future of Dust. What is it like to know—whether looking up at birds in the sky or down from a rapidly descending balloon? How does one sort out or is forced to sort out, the ethics of a situation? All of us, in fact, like Scoresby, may drift above our worlds, but, sometimes, we have to land, feet on the ground. And, finally, what is it like to read—the world around us, the words before us, the postcards, games or ephemera presented along with the books. As the preface to *Lyra's Oxford* states, "There are many things we haven't yet learned how to read." It's learning how to interpret a story—your own or someone's else's, the text or the artifacts attached to it—that is the process by which you become more human and the process by which Dust is increased in the world. *Lyra's Oxford* and *Once Upon a Time in the North* are about bringing vision into play and bringing reality down to earth. And earth—whatever earth we have, the only earth we have—is Dust, covered with stories, renewed by each narrative interaction. Dust thou art and unto Dust thou shalt return. That return is, in Pullman's literary world, not inevitable death but necessary revitalizing.

PART III

All the History of Human Life Has Been a Struggle between Wisdom and Stupidity.

8

Cuts Like a Knife

RANDALL E. AUXIER

> I don't like that knife.
>
> —IOREK BYRNISON in *The Amber Spyglass*, p. 160

> Wearily Lyra sighed; she had forgotten how roundabout scholars could
> be. It was difficult to tell them the truth when a lie would have been
> so much easier for them to understand.
>
> —*The Golden Compass*, p. 85

Methinks that Master Pullman has *known* a scholar or two.
Tiresomely roundabout. We ask the most annoyingly precise questions, and we insist that everything make genuine sense, so if you
don't want to watch your own story melt away into contradictions
and paradoxes, you'd best avoid us.

But in this case, it's too late, Philip. We found you. And not only
scholars, but the most tiresome lot of them . . . philosophers. No
one has more patience with hair-splitting than we do, and no, we
won't settle for lies. Fortunately, we're only having some fun at the
moment, so we (or at least I) ought to be able to loosen up a little
for the space of one chapter.

What in the Worlds Is He Talking About?

His Dark Materials is brimming with philosophical themes and
ideas. One friend of mine, himself a novelist, remarked that Book
III (*The Amber Spyglass*) is so long because Pullman was more
interested in developing the philosophical ideas than he was in
moving the plot along. Probably so. But even allowing this, I don't

think it's quite right to think of Pullman as a *philosopher*, even secondarily. He wisely does not even *try* to solve all of the problems he explores, and indeed, he doesn't make any serious effort to be logically consistent in presenting them.

For example, in Book I Pullman has Lord Asriel describe the splitting of worlds this way:

> Now that world [in the Aurora], and every other universe, came about as a result of possibility. Take the example of tossing a coin: it can come down heads or tails, and we don't know before it lands which way it's going to fall. If it comes down heads, that means the possibility of its coming down tails has collapsed. Until that moment the two possibilities were equal. But on another world, it does come down tails. And when that happens, the two worlds split apart. I'm using the example of tossing a coin to make it clearer. In fact, these possibility collapses happen at the level of elementary particles, but they happen in just the same way: one moment, several things are possible, the next moment only one happens, and the rest don't exist. Except that other worlds have sprung into being, on which they *did* happen." (*The Golden Compass*, pp. 376–77)

But in Book III, Pullman, narrating a tough decision to be made by Will Parry, says:

> Will considered what to do. When you choose one way out of many, all the ways you don't take are snuffed out like candles, as if they'd never existed. At the moment, all Will's choices existed at once. But to keep them all in existence meant doing nothing. He had to choose after all. (*The Amber Spyglass*, p. 12)

That's it. No mention of other worlds springing into being in which each alternative *was* respectively taken. Looking at the two passages, anybody can see that we can't have it both ways. At least sometimes (or maybe even always), *making* a choice either creates a new parallel world (first quote), *or* it doesn't (second quote). If our choices only *sometimes* create new worlds, it would be nice to know when that happens and why. Pullman is unhelpfully silent on the matter.

Yet, looking at the second passage, if there really is no other world in which Will's various other choices *are* acted on, then it undermines the premise of the whole trilogy, because there wouldn't *be* other worlds for Will to cut into. On the other hand, I'm sure you can see what a mess it would be to try to tell a story where each choice by every character resulted in a new alternative narrative thread, describing the events in which each genuine option *really* happened in *some* world. In fact—unless you're Stephen King—telling any story *requires* that you exclude all the stories that you're *not* telling at that moment, right?

That's all well and good. We're telling the story we're telling, and not telling the story we aren't telling, and that is both wise and necessary. We may tell a story about many worlds without trying to tell about every single one. So, actually things don't get too tedious or paradoxical until one supposes that we might *travel* between these contrary worlds that (at least sometimes) get created when we make a choice, or when a coin comes down heads. Lord Asriel says, in the same conversation as above:

> No one thought it would ever be possible to cross from one universe to another. That would violate fundamental laws, we thought. Well, we were wrong; we learned to *see* the world up there. If light can cross, so can we. . . . And I'm going to that world beyond the Aurora, because I think that's where all the Dust in this universe comes from. (*The Golden Compass*, pp. 376–77)

The issue is really "travel." Such travel, philosophically speaking, requires four ideas: (1) something that remains *identifiable* while (2) *moving* through some arrangement of (3) *space*, in some (4) duration of *time*. We can generate all sorts of paradoxes regarding any of these four ideas, once we have that subtle knife. And you've seen plenty of movies where these problems come up.

Just as a teaser, consider this: Whenever Will and Lyra make a bad choice, why don't they just use the knife to cut right over into the nearby world (that recently sprang into being) in which they made a better choice? Well, part of the problem is that they would, I assume, encounter the doubles of themselves, and that would get complicated in a hurry. Pretty soon we'd have a whole herd of Wills and Lyras, making better choices for sure but increasingly bothersome to feed and clothe. This paradox calls into question (1) above, since we now do not know how to *identify* the "thing" (Will or Lyra) that has *moved* through *space* and *time*. Who is the real Will or Lyra? The hungriest? The best dressed?

Pullman briefly considers this prospect in Book II, when he has Lyra contemplate whether there might be "another Lyra" in *Will's* Oxford. "A chill ran down her back, and mouse-shaped Pantalaimon shivered in her pocket. She shook herself; there were mysteries enough without imagining more" (SK, p. 74). So Pullman leaves the question open, and proceeds to tell a story in which "transworld identity" is unique—only one Lyra, one Will, one Mrs. Coulter, and so on. He evades the question rather than answering it. That's fine for a novelist.

Similarly, one could wonder why Pullman decides to keep day and night constant across the various worlds—night-time in Cittàgazze corresponds with night-time in both Oxfords, and similarly with the seasons, and so forth. I see no reason why this has to be a constant, but it does avoid troublesome questions. So when I picture the earth hurtling through space, I suppose that I need to imagine billions more right on top of it, in other dimensions of possibility, but all of them are in the same place as far as their turning and orbiting goes. So, that is one way of handling (3) above, space. But if we imagine that there's just one world that, for some reason, falls a little behind in its rotations or its orbit, could Will still cut into it? How? Does the knife do space travel? And if so, what time would it be when we stepped through there? I have trouble enough understanding what happens when I cross the International Date Line in *this* world.

I would also point out that Pullman likes to keep spaces constant, so that whatever world exists on top of another world shares the same constant space in a different dimension of possibility. He assumes that when Will and Lyra sit on the "same bench" in their different Oxfords, they remain "close." That's how Pullman wants us to imagine it.

But don't think about this too much, even on Pullman's terms. It may begin to dawn on you that somehow Lyra *walks* into the hills above Cittàgazze from the far north of her world, over Asriel's bridge, while Will finds a window into the same city from *his* Oxford, which is supposed to be right on top of Lyra's Oxford, which is a thousand miles from where she walked over Lord Asriel's bridge. My advice is not to expect consistency in these matters. It will simply frustrate your mind and spoil your enjoyment of the story. It's best to evade, as Pullman does. There are mysteries enough without imagining more, as he puts it.

The Barnard-Stokes Business

Such evasions may serve a novelist well enough, but they won't do for a physicist or a philosopher. We are wearisome and roundabout. In Lyra's world, a pair of trouble-makers, "renegade experimental theologians" named Barnard and Stokes, suggested a theory that Pullman clearly likes. He calls it the "Barnard-Stokes business." In *our* world, the physicist Hugh Everett (1930–1982) proposed this same hypothesis of the "plurality of worlds" in 1957. He was no renegade—he actually did top secret work for the US Department of Defense—but he was trying to provide an interpretation for some unsettling implications about the collapse of wave functions in quantum physics. He wasn't at all interested in the possibility of *travel* among complementary worlds, or even whether such worlds are "actual places." That is a question for metaphysics, not physics.

And some metaphysician was eventually bound to try to defend the idea that such possible worlds really do exist. Most notoriously, a philosopher named David K. Lewis (1941–2001) tried to argue for it in a book called *On the Plurality of Worlds*. I have no reason to think Pullman read this book or even knows about it, but it was widely discussed by philosophers, and it still is. But Pullman constantly violates Lewis's restrictions on the idea of many worlds. And Pullman makes arguments of the sort that Lewis happily destroys. In particular, Lewis insists that even though the many worlds actually exist, they are "causally independent" of one another—the very view of which Lord Asriel says "we were wrong." What Lewis means is that the worlds have no effect on one another. Thus, travel among them is impossible. It is unlikely enough to defend the *actuality* of all (or some) possible worlds, but it is simply crazy to suggest viable *travel* among them, Lewis thinks. In this instance, I'll have to side with the commonsense of the despised Church in Asriel's world. It's not that Barnard and Stokes are heretics, it's that they aren't talking sense. Anyway, in our world, the "Barnard-Stokes business" might be called the "Everett-Lewis business." It's out there, and you can learn about it if you want to.

A Shout-out

Church and Everett-Lewis be damned, for Pullman there are *lots* of ways to get from one world to another. Consider some. Witches "know" about the other worlds, but do not traditionally visit them. *How* they "know" isn't clarified (I have a theory about that in Chapter 1 of this volume). Yet, even just "knowing" requires that something permits exchange or *communication* of some sort among the worlds. And remember that the Gallivespian lodestone resonator also communicates across worlds by quantum entanglement, and the alethiometer somehow reads across worlds. Add to that: a single hair of Lyra's remains vitally connected to its owner, even if she's wandering around the world of the dead.

Then there's Dust. Assuming that Dust (1) moves the alethiometer needles, (2) interacts with Mary Malone's computer apparatus, and (3) moves the sticks of the *I Ching* (whether in Will's world or in that of the mulefa), then Dust also somehow communicates across worlds or exists in many at the same time. These happenings indicate that the many worlds may be *causally* connected. Whether things like quantum entanglement and the non-localized exchange of information require "causation" remains a hot topic among philosophers and physicists, but it's enough to be aware that *some* intelligible connection (whether causal or not) is involved in communication. These worlds *can* affect one another.

A Pause for the Cause

Communication isn't the only effect of one world on another. For Pullman, angels can travel among the worlds, both physically and using imagination, and affect things. And one can open a huge doorway by harnessing the energy of Dust released in intercision. One can also make a bomb so powerful as to detonate it in one world and blow a hole through *another* world, a hole so big that it opens onto the Abyss. And apparently there are "cracks" everywhere after that, in which all the worlds are bleeding vital force into the Abyss. These connections among worlds seem pretty "causal" to me.

And finally, there's the knife—our particular point of interest, if you'll tolerate my pun. So not only does Pullman allow us to remain *who-we-are* as we move among worlds, he devises a bunch of different ways that such travel might be carried out. We could spend all our time thinking about any one of these—for example, the use of imagination for traveling among worlds, described by the Angel Xaphania near the end of Book III, could easily occupy us for a whole chapter. I want to cut to the quick. I want to be the bearer of my own subtle knife (and keep all my fingers), and use it to reveal a "cosmos" in Pullman's ponderings, because I think that *his* knife helps us see how it all fits together.

Cosmos

I've already said a few words about physics and metaphysics, but philosophers and physicists also share another word: cosmology. Obviously physics is concerned with the physical world, and metaphysics includes all the problems of physics and also questions about whether (and how) non-physical entities or energies might or might not exist, and how they might affect or influence physical things. For example, is an "idea" a physical thing? It's not obvious. Metaphysics concerns itself with questions such as whether the "mind" is just the same thing as the "brain," with no remainder, on the one hand, or whether I might have an idea in my mind that can be correlated with some sort of physical process in my brain, but the two are *not* the same thing, on the other hand.

But in addition to all this, philosophers and physicists also discuss cosmology, which is the science (or study) of *order* (*kosmos* is just the Greek word for order). In modern times, this has meant the study of the order of *nature*. Most scientists and philosophers believe that "nature" is an ultimate category—nothing beyond nature really exists. So studying the order of nature is the same as studying *all* order. Anyone can see that nature is complex, so the study of cosmology has to do with grasping how the various forms of order we find in nature are best explained. Cosmology is neither quite the same as physics or metaphysics, but it uses both, just as far as they reveal patterns of order.

For example, *time* has a characteristic "order," a "before and after," a sort of durational arrow of cumulative flow. And *space* has a characteristic order, in which everything must be some*where*, a sort of localizability that can be measured with instruments or modeled with geometries. And perhaps *consciousness* has an order as well—it's one type of temporal process that is spontaneous and *intentional*, directed toward objects in space and time *other than itself*. And so on. These are just three examples of types of order, and cosmology tries to say how they fit together into one order. Our popular Big Bang theory is a bit of cosmology. When we speak of cosmology, then, we're concerned with how *all* the things that really exist are ordered in relation to each other, how the fundamental forces we discover combine to create all that we see, feel, and experience. Needless to say, it's not rocket science or brain surgery—it's far worse. Rocket science and brain surgery are pretty clear and simple by comparison.

And Chaos

The ancients had lots of different cosmologies, so you would find many different answers to questions about what is the sky, where did the earth come from, what is a person, what is a soul, what are the stars, how were people created, and what are the gods. The ancients also usually had an idea like "chaos," which was either an absence of order, or more commonly the power of disorder or the destruction of order. These ancient cosmologies are expressed in stories and myths that say what sorts of things exist by telling how they came into being. Sometimes also there are stories about how and when things pass out of being.

In the book of Genesis, when God is intent on whipping up a cosmos, "the earth is without form and void." That's Hebrew chaos. The Greeks thought of the primal waters around the whole world as chaos—they called these waters *okeanos*. Pretty much everyone seems to agree that chaos is "deep" and very much to be avoided, so it's a relief when God or Cronos tells the *Abyss* to behave itself and stay over there where it belongs, away from us and our order.

A Menagerie

Philip Pullman's cosmology is, frankly, a mish-mash of ancient and modern ideas about what types of things exist and in what order. But let me offer just the simplest list to give you a sense of what we are dealing with. According to Pullman, at least the following types of *conscious* entities exist:

1. **humans (this may or may not include witches),**

2. **ordinary animals (like Moxie, Will's cat),**

3. **talking Animals (like armored bears and arctic foxes),**

4. **night-ghasts (a type of spirit who haunt Lyra in Book I; may include Nälkäinens, Breathless Ones, the old ghost at Godstow, and the bad spirits pinned to the clockwork of the buzzing spies),**

5. **cliff-ghasts (ancient dragon-like noxious beings),**

6. **ghosts (such as are found in the world of the dead),**

7. **daemons (this may or may not include "souls"),**

8. angels (apparently a different kind of spirit than the various ghasts),

9. Dust, or matter (which "loves Dust").

There are also some beings that may be peculiar to the world of the dead, such as (10) harpies, (11) deaths, and (12) that uncooperative Boatman. And there are the mulefa, whom we are told are "people," so one assumes that they are, in the relevant sense, the same sort of thing as humans, but we are not told whether they have daemons inside them, or ghosts, or deaths. Then we have to add (13) the specters (also apparently the same as "Windsuckers"). We learn near the end of the trilogy that specters are little pieces of the Abyss, set loose in the world by the unwise (sinful? forbidden?) act of cutting through from one world to another. The specters are conscious (Pullman calls them "malevolent"—which literally means having a bad will) and they can be commanded (by Mrs. Coulter, who also teaches them they can fly). So here the suggestion is that (14) the Abyss as a whole may also be *conscious* in some sense, since the *parts* of it are conscious. As you can see, I've been tiresomely scholarly in listing Pullman's entities. There are probably some I've missed, of course, but this will be enough for a sketch of a cosmology.

Panpsychism

There you have at least fourteen types of conscious beings that can exist more or less independently, or separate conscious modes of existing. It would take a good while to sort them all out. As a list, this is not a cosmology, it's an "ontology," which is to say, it's an account of *what* exists without much regard for *how* they exist, and their levels of being and their origins and relations and dependencies upon one another. I have listed only the *conscious* beings because, as far as I can tell, Pullman intends to occupy a position philosophers call "panpsychism," which is the view that everything that really exists *is conscious*. So the idea that "dead matter" exists is an idea Pullman rejects. That is also part of the reason I am inclined to say that the Abyss is in some way conscious (and malevolent).

Panpsychism is not a popular view among philosophers these days. But some very famous ones in the past have defended panpsychism. These days there are simply oceans of philosophers who believe that *some* things are conscious and some *just aren't*. This conviction provides them with endless swimming (and treading and drowning) as they marvel at how *anything* can be conscious, since they think most things *aren't*, but a few things (like philosophers), clearly *are*. These ocean swimmers are called dualists. I don't like them. Pullman skips over these vast and tedious waters and just dives into the small pond of current philosophers who think that everything is conscious, and who just smile at the idea of "dead matter."

I think we can safely say that all of Pullman's worlds are conscious, and they all rest delicately above the Abyss, and the Abyss doesn't *like it*, which is why all those worlds are in danger of falling back into a sort of chaos. In the Abyss these tiny drops of awareness are powerless to connect, communicate, build, create, even though they still "exist." This is chaos for Pullman: a kind of awareness that is isolated and alone, which is to say, awareness trapped and powerless amid the complete absence of beauty.

Lost in Space(Time)

So, given the list of conscious beings above, all kinds of questions arise. For example, why do ghosts hold together in the world of the dead (whether they like it or not), but dissolve in the "open air"? Why can some ghosts *resist* dissolving in Asriel's Republic, and why can they "fight" with specters? What would happen to Lyra if Pantalaimon, accidentally got swatted when he was moth-formed? Where did the night-ghasts come from, the ones that haunted Lyra after she switched the coins betokening their daemons? If they had been ghosts, they'd be trapped in the world of the dead, right? Do the mulefa have or need daemons? Are tualapi (those weird swan-things in the mulefa's world) animals (as their grazers clearly are)? Or are they some further order of conscious beings, like cliff-ghasts? Why do they obey Father Gomez? And Mrs. Coulter teaches the specters to fly. How can a specter *learn* something? Do they have individual memories, a social order, rules of behavior, communication skills that can be improved with effort?

This could go on forever, rather tediously, as we try to compile all the types of beings and all their interactions—who can *communicate* with whom, who can *hurt* whom, and so on. We need a method of sorting it all out. Normally a good way to begin to put things in order in cosmology is to ask two questions: "When does it exist?" and "Where does it exist?" Where and when would a person expect to find whatever it is we're looking for? If you know the space and the time, you can begin to tell a story about how it all fits together, by hypothesizing what *caused* what. Here we always assume that what comes *later* is caused by something *earlier* (time), and we expect to find things that cause one another in close *proximity* (space). Such is the structure of standard cosmologies.

But this method won't work for sorting out Pullman's cosmology. That's because he has taken a certain delight in messing around with our ordinary ideas about space, time, and causality. He explicitly holds constant a *few* features of space and time and cause, but not reliably. In his naughtiest moment, he actually has Will use the knife to cut through *time*, by just a few moments, when he and Lyra and the Gallivespians are looking for the world of the dead. Will *had been* using the knife as a tool to cut across spatial dimensions, or dimensions of possibility, but then Pullman just teases us by having it cut through a few minutes of *time*. How wicked.

In terms of space, it's good to remember that Pullman also has the worlds of dreaming and waking in close spatial relation, as when Serafina Pekkala projects into Mary Malone's dream so as to awaken her without frightening her, and Lee Scoresby accompanies John Parry on the mission to destroy Zeppelins in his dreaming state. Pullman also has Mary do something akin to astral projection from her platform high among the wheel-pod trees. These are not the sorts of space-time-cause relations that we can explain with modern physics, so our ordinary assumptions about the relative constancy of space and time and cause will not help us tell the story of Pullman's cosmology.

Mephistopheles Is Not My Name

This slippage of space, time and cause is to be expected, however. Pullman is no doctrinaire defender of modern science. If anything, he sees the scientific revolution as a moment when humankind, in many worlds, lost its way. He explicitly dates the time when things start to go "wrong" as being three hundred years ago, when Newton was framing his physics in our world, the Guild of the Philosophers was creating the subtle knife in Cittàgazze, the experimental theologians were devising the alethiometer in Lyra's world, and the wheel-pod trees began to fail in the world of the mulefa. Pullman is toying with the idea that modern science, and its fetish for technology, is a sort of Faustian bargain human beings made with *themselves* (not the devil) by being overly curious and greedy for knowledge. Every world has suffered from their unwise quest for a kind of truth that destroys beauty. This is not even the fault of the Church, in Pullman's tale—it's one of the few things he does *not* blame on the Church. The point is that trying to use a cosmology of space, time, cause, and nature to grasp this cosmology will not work.

Another Day in Paradise

Instead, we need to remember that there is a certain "mythic" cast to the trilogy that reminds us of some basic features of mythic consciousness (and of dream consciousness), which need not obey the laws of space, time and cause we take for granted these days. If I had to name a single cosmology from history that is most akin to Pullman's it would be John Milton's, which has the same odd mix of modern science and mythic beings, and it offers the same judgment of humans when they get too curious about nature. Of course, unlike Pullman, Milton (as far as I can tell) actually *believed* in all these sorts of mythic beings. That's hard to do these days, but the stories still tug at our feelings. A lot of people still believe in angels.

In Pullman's universe you can't even pin down identity, let alone space and time. People *do* remain more or less *who* they are from one world to the next, but identity is *plural* in Pullman's cosmos. He has a favorite strategy for handling the issue of plural identity, which is to give a separate identity to every *layer* of the self he can imagine. Every time he catches himself imagining a basic layer of self-experience, he externalizes and personifies it. So, for example, our human *souls* become daemons, and a bear's armor is an external soul of a different sort, and our *deaths* are outside of us, but always nearby. The insects of the Gallivespians are external manifestations of their nurturing instincts and their clan idenities (Salmakkia feeds hers on her own blood at one point, yuck). This is Pullman's standard move: externalize, personify.

If we had eyes to see every level of conscious existence at once, and we saw Lyra coming down the High Street in Oxford, we would behold a veritable crowd: her regular body, the small amount of Dust she attracts, her death, her daemon, her ghost, and, I assume, the part of her that is spirit or mind (the part that can become an angel, if someone helps her like Balthamos helped Baruch). Maybe we would also see some witch oil. Who knows? And then, having externalized and personified all these aspects of the self, Pullman likes to pull the various identities apart—just like the golden monkey does with bats and Gallivespians, and whatever it can get hold of. Pullman uses his imagination to part children from their daemons, and Baruch from Balthamos, and in death, he cuts off ghosts from their physical bodies, and finally, he tears apart Lyra and Will, banishes them forever to different worlds. It seems like a cruel experiment, actually, to spend one's time wondering what a person would be without his spirit, or without his soul, and so on. But that is part of the clue to figuring out how Pullman's cosmology really works, what principle is really behind it. It's about cutting things.

Rock, Paper, Scissors

When you can't quite count on space, time and causality to give you the order of the universe, you have to start looking around for other ideas that help in grouping things in order. It's like a game of rock, paper, scissors, which is a complete triad of dependency relations. You know the game: rock smashes scissors, scissors cut paper, paper covers rock. There are three *ways* of being: smashing, cutting, covering. And we have three *types* of entities that do these things, each being limited by one of the others. It's a perfect cosmology.

If you go back before the time when we decided cosmology was about space, time and cause, you discover that philosophers have been playing rock, paper, scissors for the whole of Western history. Their three favorite entities are the Good (which is sort of a rock), the True (which is like a pair of scissors), and the Beautiful (like the paper), but people don't agree on the rules or the functions or the ways that each limits the other. Plato started the game, and he enjoyed playing all three. Ever since then, philosophers have tended to favor one and to try to get it to do the work of both of the others.

In the last hundred years or so, the philosophers who like the True have had all the power. The defenders of the Good, after a brief period of disorientation, have been climbing back into the conversation, but the believers in the Beautiful have been both cut and smashed. They had their heyday in the Renaissance, with a flurry of further prominence during the two generations dominated by Romanticism. The lovers of the Good owned the Victorian era. Now we have these boring philosophers who only care about Truth. If I had to guess, I would predict that we are in for another round of dominance by the lovers of Beauty in the near future, when everyone tires of the True (the dominance of science in this case).

I'm tired of Truth myself. I'd rather be lied to, which is why I like Pullman. And in fact, Pullman is definitely one of the friends of the Beautiful. I have some sympathy for the Good, but not very much, and that is how I read Pullman too. And that is why his cosmology is difficult to understand by means of either a moral order or a scientific (or logical or epistemological) ordering. And thus, we have our clue. The Pullman cosmology obeys aesthetic principles, the logic of imagination and feeling, *not* the order of good and evil *or* of truth and lies (for more about those types of order, see my other essay in this volume).

The Beauty in the Beast

Aesthetic cosmologies follow the order of images and possibilities, what images *can suggest*. Here we are not very interested in *arguments* and what they logically *imply*, or in *moral principles* and what they *demand*. Cosmologies of the True and the Good are built around *necessary* relations—not what *can* be, but what *must* be. Cosmologies of the True and the Good are stern and humorless companions. You wouldn't tolerate a novel, or a movie, or even a song that was just one long series of logical implications or moral commands. People who read the Bible as just one long series of moral requirements are missing a lot about the book—it's interesting literature. People who read the Bible as an explanation of the natural world, like a bit of science that is literally true, are very much to be pitied. Imagine being that unimaginative. I just can't.

One of the coolest things about aesthetic cosmologies is that they are built around *possibility* instead of necessity—what *can* we imagine, and what *can* we do in imagination? The cosmology of the Beautiful does not want to be told that "you can't really do that, it isn't physically possible," or "you ought not do that, it's morally wrong." And this is really the clue we need, to make sense of Pullman's cosmos. What's possible and what's impossible in his story? Doing useful philosophy really depends on finding the right question and asking it in the right way. Simply being *aware* that cosmologies *can* proceed in different ways is important background knowledge, but until you have the question firmly before you, you have no direction.

Scholars are roundabout, but they usually get where they are going. I knew what my question was at the outset, but I only now share it with you, dear reader. The question is: what *will* the subtle knife cut and what *won't* it cut? Having settled on the idea that Pullman's universe is governed by aesthetic rules, it's easy to see that he's worried about possibility, not necessity. That is why he doesn't care to give us consistent physics or to solve impossible moral dilemmas with some set of clear rules.

Searching through the universe of Pullman's imagination for a key to the kingdom is not difficult. Three powerfully suggestive images jump out immediately: (1) *The Golden Compass* (the alethiometer); (2) *The Subtle Knife*; and (3) *The Amber Spyglass* (that is, the idea of learning to see Dust). I wonder: where might a semi-observant person get the idea that just these three images are important? Duh. In any case, thinking about these three and asking what is *possible* for them provides us with our rock, paper and scissors: the aesthetic order of Pullman's universe. We need only ask what is possible for these things and what is impossible, what they'll *do* and what they *won't do*.

Dust

Obviously, Dust *moves* the alethiometer. That's one thing it *can do*. If Mary Malone had been kind enough to point her spyglass in the right direction, I'm sure she would have seen the Dust dance. But it's also clear that Dust has limits. It can't do just anything. Its main limit is that it can organize itself into something communicative *only* in the presence of an appropriate intention. How this works would be a long story. Basically, Mary Malone thinks that the human brain had just the right sort of sympathy and resonance to permit Dust to organize itself in ways that communicate. Without that, Dust cannot become conscious of itself. This is not science, it's an invention of the imagination.

So even though Dust can express itself through computers and the *I Ching* and the alethiometer, it is not a powerful force at all. We have to *expect* to see it before we can make use of its benefits.

The benefits are: truth, goodness, and most of all, beauty. So when we understand the word "moves" in "Dust moves the alethiometer," I think we mean "moves" in a physical, a moral, *and* an aesthetic sense. Something "moves" us when we experience our whole moral and physical and emotional existence at the same time. That is what Dust does, it "moves" things that are susceptible to being moved, and that *want* to be moved. That includes the alethiometer, but not the knife.

The Compass

The relationship between the alethiometer and the knife is a little harder to understand, but properly used, the alethiometer actually *guides* the knife. That's one thing it *can* do. In an important conversation, as Lyra and Will are wandering around in Will's Oxford, he is unsettled at the idea that Lyra can use the alethiometer to know what she shouldn't know, to invade privacy. Will says: "that's enough. You've got no right to look into my life like that. Don't ever do that again. That's just spying." But Lyra's all important answer is:

> I know when to stop asking. See, the alethiometer's like a person, almost. I sort of know when it's going to be cross or when there's things it doesn't want me to know. I kind of feel it. . . . This en't like a private peep show. If I done nothing but spy on people, it'd stop working. I know that as well as I know my own Oxford. (*The Subtle Knife*, pp. 104–05)

What the alethiometer *can't do* is tell the future, but that isn't as important as what it *won't* do. In the very next moment the question is raised about whether Will's father is still alive, an absolutely crucial question—and Lyra doesn't ask the alethiometer *because* Will doesn't direct her to do so. *Why* Will doesn't ask her to consult the device is hard to understand, except that he is consistent in this attitude throughout the whole story. He is struggling with freedom and fate, and he resolutely chooses *not* to know all sorts of things he *could* know, because he wants to preserve his *sense* of freedom (not his freedom itself, just his sense of it). So he chooses to preserve an aesthetic feature of his life, the feeling of acting freely, instead of knowing morally or scientifically what he "must" do.

The alethiometer, however, works with and through its interpreter, and so long as she accepts Will's guidance, the instrument works to the "best" (meaning the most beautiful) purposes. That purpose is saving Dust, not because it is good or true, but because it is the basis of all that it beautiful in the world. This tells us what is possible and impossible for the alethiometer, and what we mean by saying that the knife "guides" it. We mean that Will the bearer of the power, tells Lyra when to use it and when not to, for the most part. And Lyra wisely obeys. Thus, the alethiometer *submits* to the knife.

Cut to the Chase

But the all important and pivotal cosmological function is that of the knife itself. If you can tolerate an analogy for a moment, I will clarify. If I had been writing this essay on Tolkien's *Lord of the Rings*, I would have made almost the same argument about aesthetic cosmologies, because I think he and Pullman are kindred spirits (C.S. Lewis is different; his cosmology is clearly moral). But if this were about Tolkien, I would have analyzed all the rings— nine for the humans, seven for the dwarves, three for the elves, and then, the One Ring, the Ring of Power—to find them and in the darkness bind them. Clearly Tolkien's cosmology is symbolized in what becomes of these rings, and one is at the center.

The subtle knife is like that for Pullman. It plays the part of the one ring, which is the reason it has to be destroyed, in the end (and that is an old trope in imaginative literature, that the power that tempts us must be destroyed). I am quite certain that Pullman is giving a nod to Tolkien when he has Will destroy the knife, and when he has so many characters say that it "never should have been made," and when he places its origin in a Tower in a land that has fallen into ruin. I think Pullman makes it clear enough that the knife is the center of his cosmology. But an especially revealing passage is worth quoting, since it brings together Pullman's panpsychism and cosmology all at once. Iorek Byrnison is speaking:

> I don't like that knife. I fear what it can do. I have never known anything so dangerous. . . . The harm it can do is unlimited. It would have been infinitely better if it had never been made. . . . With it you can do strange things. What you don't know is what the knife does on its

own. Your intentions may be good. The knife has intentions too. . . . The intentions of a tool are what it does. A hammer intends to strike, a vise intends to hold fast, a lever intends to lift. They are what it is made for. But sometimes a tool may have other uses that you don't know. Sometimes in doing what you intend, you also do what the knife intends, without knowing. (*The Amber Spyglass*, p. 161)

Even ordinary tools have intentions. Lyra tries to talk the bear into fixing the knife with a fairly lame argument, but the bear is moved only by whether the alethiometer recommends fixing it. Thus, there is a sense in which the alethiometer has a power over the knife's continued existence. This completes the circle of rock, paper, scissors, but there is more to be observed. The alethiometer's power is not ultimate because we don't *know* the knife's intentions, or how to handle them. But, like the alethiometer, the knife needs a human actor to carry out its intentions, and like the alethiometer, only the *right sort* of human can use it.

That actually makes our quest for the cosmic order of Pullman's universe a lot easier. All we have to do is look at our ontology of conscious beings, all fourteen of them, and ask "what's *possible* for the knife, and what's *impossible?*" You can have a hell of a lot of fun going back and doing this now. I won't do the whole thing. I just want to call your attention to some really interesting stuff that tumbles out of this. The *impossibilities*, what the knife *cannot* do, are far more revealing than what it *can* do. But let's look at what it *can* do first.

In the right hands, the knife will cut the bear's armor, it cuts through space and time (and that's a heck of a trick), one assumes that it will kill or damage pretty much anything on the list of beings, with a few interesting exceptions. It wards off specters and harpies but we don't know whether it can kill them. The knife kills cliff-ghasts, and certainly could kill ordinary animals, talking animals, humans, witches, and daemons.

There are a number of interesting open questions, like whether the knife can affect night-ghasts and ghosts. And I wanted to use that knife on the creepy Boatman on the lake of the dead, but Pullman has the old fellow claim he can't be hurt by it. I would like to find out for sure. I also don't know whether one could kill one's own death with it, but I suppose not. Death is already dead, right? Since it is called the "god-destroyer," one assumes that the knife can kill angels. And the knife can cut Dust. The energy in Dust is released not only by the knife, but by a blade less fine: the guillotine at Bolvangar can do it, so certainly the subtle knife can. But the ultimate power the knife has is to sever the delicate membrane that protects the many worlds from the Abyss.

A Matter of Love

Pullman is silent on the issue of whether there was a creator who first set the Abyss (Chaos) and the Cosmos in their separate domains. He allows that perhaps there *was* a creator, but the Authority was not the Creator. All we can know is that the most powerful thing the knife can do is to rejoin Cosmos to Chaos, such that Chaos comes in (as specters) and Dust (the basis of conscious order) flows out. And if Iorek Byrnison is right, then this is what the knife *intends*: to *undo* the work of the creator. But we also have a clue as to what is powerful enough to *smash* the knife: love. Thus, when we know what Pullman means by "love," we know what's stronger than the knife, stronger than the golden compass, and stronger than Dust.

Both times that the knife is broken, it is the power of Will's love that does it: for his mother in the first instance, and for Lyra in the second. But Pullman's ideas about love are not Romantic, they are cosmic, aesthetic ideas, summed up in his statement that "Matter loved Dust. It didn't want to see it go" (AS, p. 404). A number of philosophers in history have spoken of "love" in this way, notably St. Augustine and St. Thomas Aquinas. One finds John Milton speaking this way also. The traditional cosmologies of love are usually Christian. But we all know that Pullman has little sympathy for *that*.

The philosopher whose ideas about love most closely correspond to Pullman's are those of the American philosopher Charles Sanders Peirce (1839–1914). The reason Peirce's view is closer to Pullman's than the traditional Christian cosmologies is basically because Peirce, like Pullman, is an evolutionist. I will not weigh you down with a long description of Peirce's cosmology, called *Agapasticism* (after the Greek word *agape*, love). Suffice it to say that this is an aesthetic cosmology, in which everything that exists is built on mutual feeling. Here is a little sample:

> Three modes of evolution have been brought before us: evolution by fortuitous variation, evolution by mechanical necessity, and evolution by creative love. . . . the mere propositions that absolute chance, mechanical necessity, and the law of love, are severally operative in

the cosmos, may receive the names of *tychism, anancism,* and *apgapism*. (*Philosophical Writings of Peirce*, Dover, 1955, p. 364)

Peirce believes the universe allows all three types of evolution to exist, but he doesn't think all three modes are equally operative in what exists. Agapism is the more comprehensive proposition. It accounts for "the bestowal of spontaneous energy by the parent upon the offspring, and . . . the disposition of the latter to catch the general idea of those about it and thus to subserve the general purpose. . . In the very nature of things, the line of demarcation between the three modes of evolution is not perfectly sharp. That does not prevent its being quite real." Peirce carries on about all this, brilliantly, for quite a few pages. If you now look back to where we began with this chapter, you'll see that Pullman handles evolution by chance and by mechanical necessity as being modes that work at a lower level of explanation than his idea of "love." So he is consistent, he just isn't interested in *logical* consistency. He plies the trade of the story-teller, which requires aesthetic and imaginative rules, not logical, scientific or moral ones.

But Peirce is a little further down that same path. He actually reconciles, with logic and science, these different modes of evolution using viable philosophical arguments—although it isn't as much fun to read as Pullman is. Now, I know you have probably never heard of Peirce, and I have no reason at all to think that Pullman has ever read him. And you might think, "well, other philosophers and scientists and even theologians must think Peirce is daft, to defend such ideas as 'evolutionary love.'" But that would be very far from the case. Peirce's influence has been steadily growing for many years, and even his critics stand in almost perfect awe of his intellect and his learning, which are only recently beginning to come into common understanding. You might want to read a little ways into Peirce's philosophy, since I know you like Pullman's ideas.

My point is that if you follow Pullman's knife right into the world of contemporary cosmology, you might be surprised to find out how viable his most central ideas are. You don't need to travel to other worlds or believe in them. All you need is an open mind and a fair command of the game of rock, paper, scissors. If you don't believe me, check your own alethiometer. As Lyra once said, "I'm the best liar there ever was. But I en't lying to you, and I never will" (SK, p. 103).

9

Is Lyra Free Enough to Be a Hero?

NICOLAS MICHAUD

Our hero, Lyra, is the object of a prophecy. It was prophesied by the witches that she would save the world. In fact, this prophecy is of grave concern to the Magisterium. Usually, when we think of prophecy, we think of it as predicting something that has not happened, but *will* happen. So, we may almost pity those who oppose Lyra—if the prophecy is correct, she cannot fail. Those who oppose her must fail. But, one wonders, "What does this mean for Lyra?" If her future is foretold, can she truly be said to be free? And, if she isn't free, can she truly be said to be a hero?

Generally, when we think of a hero we think of someone who, through her own choice, does what is right. A hero must overcome great obstacles and make tough decisions. Lyra has done exactly that. But, the philosophical question is, can someone who is not free really be a hero? In other words, imagine that you find out that your hero was forced to overcome those obstacles, and that those tough decisions were made for her. Can it still be said that she is a true hero? It seems that if someone's future has been predicted then that person cannot deviate from her destiny.

The first question that you have is likely, what makes you think that Lyra is not free? Well, the question of freedom is deeply affected by the nature of prophecy. Let's consider what we know about Lyra. Dr. Lanselius tells us,

> And they have spoken of a child such as this, who has a great destiny that can only be fulfilled elsewhere—not in this world, but far beyond. Without this child we shall all die. So the witches say. But she must fulfill this destiny in ignorance of what she is doing, because only in

her ignorance can we be saved. (*The Golden Compass*, Laurel-Leaf, 1995, p. 154)

This is certainly quite a responsibility to place on Lyra's shoulders. Also, notice Dr. Lanselius's use of the word 'destiny'; Lyra has a future that has been foretold for her. Although Dr. Lanselius explains that if anyone tells Lyra about the prophecy, she will fail, it seems that it is her destiny, her fate, to save the world. But, if it's her fate, then how can she fail? And, if she cannot fail, why would we praise her? It would be like praising an armored bear for having fur.

Generally, philosophers think of having freedom as having the ability to do otherwise. If I lack the ability to do other than what I am doing, it does not seem that I am free. For instance, Iorek eats Iofur's heart and we might want to say "ewwww, he should not have done that!" But if we think about what it means to be an armored bear we can argue that Iorek did not really have a choice, it is part of who he is to do as he did—he could not do otherwise. We could argue that his action was instinctual and thereby he was not free. So blaming Iorek for his action would be kind of silly, yes? Why blame Iorek for his action when he could not do otherwise? Similarly, it seems that Lyra may not be free. She cannot do other than save the world as long as no one tells her about the prophecy. So, as she cannot do otherwise, she is not free enough to be praised or blamed for us. It would be like blaming Iorek for acting due to his instinct.

What we need to consider, first, is what it means to have a destiny. Generally, when we think of destiny, we think of something that we cannot avoid. We often use it in a prophetic sense, meaning that a particular set of events must take place. The problem, though, is that since it is Lyra's destiny to save humanity, she can't she fail to do so. If her destiny must be fulfilled, then her future is fixed, and she has no real choices. Of course, we may reply that, according to the prophecy, if she learns of the prophecy then she will fail, so it isn't certain that she will succeed. This reply does not help solve the problem. There are really only two paths that Lyra can take, and neither is under her control. The first path is the one in which she stays ignorant of her role and thereby it is her destiny to save humanity. If, on the other hand, she learns of the prophecy, she will fail to save the world. Either way, it seems that she is not free: either she stays ignorant and saves humanity or she learns of the prophecy and fails to save humanity. The final conclusion, whether or not she saves humanity, does not seem to be under her control.

Lyra Saved the World, but Did She Have a Choice?

We wonder, then, "Can Lyra truly be said to be a hero?" Lyra does not learn of the prophecy too early and so she does save the world. But she had no real control over that fact. It seems as if the witches and others around her had more control over saving humanity than Lyra did. If one witch had decided to betray them all and tell Lyra, Lyra would have failed, whether she wanted to or not. But the prophecy came true and Lyra fulfilled her destiny; can a slave to destiny truly be a hero?

When someone cannot prevent an event from happening, we generally argue that she's not responsible. We don't blame Lyra for Lee Scoresby's death, nor do we hold her responsible for not saving his life. The reason why we don't is because there's nothing she could have done to save him. Similarly, we don't blame people for actions of their own if they could not avoid them. If someone has no choice but to commit an action, we don't blame the person. If someone forced you to commit a crime by using mind control, we would not blame you for the act. We wouldn't blame you because there was nothing you could do to avoid the act. So, some philosophers argue that if you are predestined to commit an act, you cannot be blamed for it. Their argument is that since there was nothing you could do to avoid the act, you should not be blamed or praised. If they are right, then Lyra should not be praised for her actions because she had no real choice but to save the world—in essence, regardless of her will, she was destined to save the world.

Harry Frankfurt, though, disagrees with this. He believes that we can be blamed for acts, even we could not have done otherwise. So, to Frankfurt, even if you are predestined to commit a particular act, you can be blamed for it. Here I will present a Frankfurt-like example to demonstrate his point.[1] Imagine that you must make a choice to either help Lyra or help the Magisterium. Imagine

---

[1] Harry Frankfurt, "Alternate Possibilities and Moral Responsibility," *Journal of Philosophy* 66 (1969), pp. 829–839.

also that Fra Pavel Rašek has found a way to control your actions. Now, given the fact that Fra Pavel is not a very brave man he doesn't want to use force to make you help the Magisterium, unless he must. So he decides to wait for the moment you make your decision; if you decide to help the Magisterium on your own, he will do nothing, but if you decide to help Lyra, he will use his power to force you to help the Magisterium instead. Notice that in this example, no matter what, you are going to help the Magisterium, either by choice or by force. We can put it very simply. Here are the facts of the case:

1. Fra Pavel can force you to do his will, but he doesn't want anyone to know.

2. If you choose to help the Magisterium without his interference, he does nothing.

3. If you choose to help Lyra, he will force you to help the Magisterium.

4. Regardless of "2" or "3," you will help the Magisterium.

5. So, isn't it true that you must to help the Magisterium, because you cannot do otherwise?

Frankfurt's point is simply this: in the case "2" that you decide to help the Magisterium and so Fra Pavel does not have to use his power, we can still blame you for your bad act *even though "5" you could not have done otherwise*. So, Frankfurt argues that you can still be held responsible even though had no other option but to help the Magisterium. In the case that you chose to help the Magisterium without Fra Pavel's intervention, he argues that we would all still hold you responsible for your action.

It seems, then, that Frankfurt is presenting us with a case that proves our original idea wrong. Normally, we say that if you cannot do other than commit a particular act, you are not praise or blameworthy for committing the act, as in the case of Fra Pavel's mind control. But, we have just imagined a case involving mind control in which you could not do otherwise but help the Magisterium and, yet, it seems that you could still be blameworthy. If you chose to help the Magisterium of your own will, even though you had only one option, to help the Magisterium, you are blameworthy, despite your lack of options.

Yet there is a popular criticism of Frankfurt's argument. Although it seems that you have only one option, to help the Magisterium, you really have two options. One option is "2" that you act of your own will to help the Magisterium, and the other option is "3" to help the Magisterium *because Fra Pavel forces you to do so.* So, isn't Frankfurt wrong? Isn't it true that you really have two choices, "2" and "3"?

This is a problem for Frankfurt because for Frankfurt to prove that we can reasonably be blamed for our actions, even when we could not do otherwise, his example must be actually of a case in which we cannot do otherwise. There is a great deal of contention amongst philosophers as to if Frankfurt's famous examples are true cases of the inability to do otherwise. In the case of my example, you cannot do otherwise than help the Magisterium, but you can do so because you choose to help them or because you are forced to do so. So it seems you have two choices. Other philosophers think it is a bit silly to consider "3" a choice because it is a matter of force. But one way to think of "3" as a choice is to see it as "forcing Fra Pavel's hand." You must help the Magisterium but you can force Fra Pavel to intervene or not to intervene. So, some think that Frankfurt's examples do not do the work that he claims they do. What this argument really does for us, though, is help us realize that we might be missing the point. Whether or not "3" is an actual choice or option it still seems that you don't have much control of the situation. Some philosophers think that is what really matters when deciding if you can be praise or blamed—not whether you can do otherwise, but how much control you have over your actions.

How Much Control Does Lyra Have?

Lyra can fail to save the world, but that failure depends on others telling her about the prophecy. As it is, it seems that if she is kept ignorant of the prophecy, she must save the world. So, although there are two options in front of her, it seems that she is not the one who has the ability to choose between them. For reasons like this another philosopher, John Martin Fischer, argues that Frankfurt's arguments point us in the right direction—control. Fischer argues that in cases like those found in Frankfurt's examples the real question is how much control you have over the choice. In the case "3" where Fra Pavel forces you to help the

Magisterium you do not have control over the choice and so you cannot be blamed. But, in the case "2" where you do choose to help the Magisterium, you still have enough control to be blame-worthy. Even if we argue that Frankfurt is wrong about how many options we have, Fischer believes he can explain why you are blameworthy in this situation. It isn't about your number of options but the reasons why you act as you do that make you praisewor-thy or blameworthy.

In order to figure out if Lyra has enough control over her situ-ation to be praised for saving the world we need to understand Fischer's account of control and responsibility. In his book, *Responsibility and Control,* with Mark Ravizza, Fischer presents his argument for how we can lack options and yet remain praisewor-thy and blameworthy. Fischer's argument is that responsibility requires that we have guidance control over our action.[2] Guidance control, unlike the way in which we normally think of control requires only that we can imagine the ability to take options. Normally, when we think of control we believe that control requires that we really can do one thing or really can do another thing. For this reason, we generally believe that responsibility walks hand in hand with two options, because control seems to require at least two options. Fischer's guidance control does not require that we can actually do one thing or another, so in the case of the Frankfurt example, it may be that despite the fact that you can only really take one action, you are still blameworthy.

So, what does Fischer mean by guidance control? Guidance control requires two things: 1) a reasons-responsive mechanism and 2) that this mechanism is your own. A reasons-responsive mechanism is your decision-making ability. We all have reasons-responsive mechanisms, we make decisions by thinking about rea-sons, and we can respond to other reasons. So, let's say you are about to go to visit your favorite friendly armored bear and then your friend reminds you that it is a very cold trip and you don't like the cold. Given this new information, you change your mind and you can give a reason for changing your mind—because you don't like the cold.

Objects like clocks do not have reasons-responsive mecha-nisms, they act, but they cannot change their action due to reasons

---

[2] John Martin Fischer and Mark Ravizza, *Responsibility and Control: A Theory of Moral Responsibility* (Cambridge University Press, 1998).

of their own. Notice that this brings in the second component of a reasons-responsive mechanism, that it be your own. If Fra Pavel somehow controls your mind, he may decide to make you do something for his reasons or force you to change your mind for other reasons, but despite the fact that he is responding to reasons, this choice is his and not *yours*. In a case of total mind control you cannot be praised or blamed for your actions according to Fischer.

In the case of Frankfurt's example, though, Fischer argues that you do have guidance control in case "2," *if you chose to help the Magisterium without Fra Pavel forcing you to do so*. If Fra Pavel forces you to help, the mechanism isn't your own and so you are absolved, but he thinks that you do have a reason-responsive mechanism, if you decide to help on your own. But, you might argue, how can it be said that I can respond to reasons? If I change my mind and try to help Lyra, Fra Pavel will force me to change my mind. You could argue that you can't actually respond to reasons and do something and decide to help Lyra. This is where Fischer argues that we need to use our imaginations. We don't need the actual ability to change our minds and take a different action; we just need to be able to imagine that there is a possible world in which we could take the other option. So, Fischer does rely on other options, but not on actual other options, just *possible* other options.

Other Worlds and Responsibility

Think of these possible worlds like the other worlds which Lyra visits.[3] We can't be sure of whether or not they actually exist, but they are possible. We can imagine that if one thing went differently in this world, then it would result in a different, possible, world. For instance, we may imagine that Philip Pullman never wrote *His Dark Materials*. Perhaps this is a sad world to imagine, but it's a possible one. In the same way, we can imagine that there are possible worlds in which we make different decisions from the ones we're making right now. There is, for instance, a possible world in which you choose to put down this book and get ice cream. There's another possible world in which you decide to take this

---

[3] See Chapter 11 in this volume for a discussion of the differences between other worlds that Lyra visits and other possible worlds in the philosophical sense.

book with you while you get ice cream. There is, yet, another possible world in which you hate ice cream and so on. Fischer argues
that it is these possible worlds that really matter when we discuss
control.

Fischer would argue that in the case of the Frankfurt example,
you don't actually have the ability to help Lyra, but there is a possible world in which Fra Pavel never discovers his mind-control
ability. This change in possible worlds never changes your ownership of your own decision. So your mechanism, whether or not Fra
Pavel is watching or is not watching, never changes. This is an
important difference from the situation in which Fra Pavel forces
you to help the Magisterium. In that case, the ownership of your
decision-making mechanism changes from your hands to his
hands. But, in the case in which he never acts and just watches,
you can remove him from decision-making procedure without any
real impact on your decision.

And so, regardless of whether or not Fra Pavel is watching, if
you make the decision to help the Magisterium without his intervention, you make the decision entirely from your own mechanism. In this way, we can use possible worlds as a way to help us
figure out whether or not a particular something is important to
the decision-making procedure. If in the case that you help the
Magisterium, Fra Pavel's existence plays no role as demonstrated
by our possible world imaginings, we can say you have guidance
control—even though you cannot actually choose the other
option.

Fischer's point, then, is a simply broken into two parts: 1) To
have control a decision of yours must be made through your own
decision making mechanism—no mind control—and 2) Even if
you, in this world, must take a particular option, if we can imagine
a possible world in which you can take the other option, and you
retain ownership of your decision making mechanism, you have
guidance control.

So, what about Lyra, then? Does she have guidance control of
her own destiny? Well, she does seem to make her decision to save
the world based on her own decision-making mechanism. It also
seems that we can imagine a world in which Lyra of her own will
chooses not to save the world. This change in possible worlds
does not change her ownership of her decision-making mechanism. So, the answer is simple: Lyra should be praised for her
heroic deeds.

Is Fischer's Control Enough to Save Lyra?

I wonder, though, if this conclusion is too hasty. Perhaps that fact that Fischer would praise Lyra for her deeds is a good reason to believe that his account is mistaken. Consider the fact that he is willing to say that Lyra is responsible for an event over which others have more control than she does. Recall that if even one person informs Lyra of the prophecy, she will fail, no matter what she does. So, while Lyra may have guidance control over her own decisions, she does not have any control over whether or not someone else decides to tell her about the prophecy. She has no more control over this than you do over the things that happened before your birth. She also has no more control over the force of the prophecy than you do over the laws of nature. So how can she be said to have any control over whether the world is actually saved? Perhaps we can praise her for choosing to try to save the world, but whether or not the world is saved doesn't rely only on her decision, it also relies on the decision of others to keep quiet about the prophecy.

Imagine one final time that you choose to help the Magisterium instead of helping Lyra. But, when we examine the reasons why you do so, we realize that you helped the Magisterium because you have been taught from birth that the Magisterium is always right and taught that you must help them in order to save everyone else. In fact, let's imagine that given your upbringing, you have no real choice but to believe the Magisterium because no one has ever presented you with any other information. Upon even more investigation, we realize that you would have chosen to help Lyra, if even one person had taught you that the Magisterium might be wrong. Doesn't your decision really hinge, then, on whether or not someone gives you that information? If we condemned you for helping the Magisterium, wouldn't you argue, "If I had any idea that the Magisterium could be wrong, I never would have helped them!" Well, then, yes it does seem that you have control and perhaps we should blame you for your decision, but it seems that you did not have control over the thing that really mattered—whether or not you were taught that the Magisterium could be wrong.

Lyra's case, may then demonstrate a flaw in Fischer's account. Perhaps Lyra can be held responsible for her choices, but can she really be praised for the final result—the saving of the world? It seems as if that event would happen regardless of her decisions and instead was dependent upon the decisions of others. Similarly, can you really be blamed for a decision of yours when that decision was depended on forces beyond your control, like in the case above? On one hand, we want to say "yes" but on the other hand we realize that in another possible world we would have acted very differently, if only one small thing were different. Shouldn't we say that whoever it is that has control over that "one small thing" is really responsible?

The final answer may simply be that we are responsible, but not by ourselves. Lyra is responsible for saving the world, but as we have discussed, the saving of the world didn't depend solely on her, it also depended on all of the others who fought and kept the prophecy secret. In the same way, you may be responsible for helping the Magisterium, but the Magisterium is also responsible for deceiving you. Responsibility need not be something that applies to only one person per event. Events in the world are dependent on the decisions of many people and each of those people likely shares in the responsibility for the event coming about. So, the next time we blame one person for something bad, like the Authority or even Metatron, perhaps we should also be seeking to blame the many people, even ourselves, who were necessary participants in bringing that event about.

Is Lyra a hero? The successes of all heroes are never solely dependent on the heroes themselves. Every hero has probably been subject to forces beyond her control and so, in the end, even though Lyra may not be solely responsible for saving the world, she's no different from any other hero in that regard. We tend to view heroes as acting by themselves, but where would any of our heroes be without all of the other less celebrated heroes who help bring about success?

Being a hero probably has less to do with single-handedly succeeding in a particular endeavor and more to do with strength of character and pursuit of good regardless of great self-sacrifice. In that way, even though Lyra had very little control over her own success, she is a hero because the choices she made, despite her control of the consequences, reflect upon her as someone who seeks to do great good, even at a great cost to herself.

10
Could the Magisterium Be Right?

NICOLAS MICHAUD

The Magisterium does many bad things. They physically mutilate children, cut children from their dæmons, and kill those who get in the way of their grand designs. There's no question that the Magisterium could improve its behavior. What I want to ask about is not their treatment of people, but their treatment of knowledge.

One of the key characteristics of the Magisterium is that they go to a great deal of effort to prevent others from knowing about Dust. The Magisterium has a monopoly on information and they want to prevent much of that information from getting out to the general public. As a matter of fact, they do what they can to prevent others from even researching Dust and other seemingly innocent things. More than anything, the Magisterium seems afraid of questions. Is this attempt to restrain the pursuit of knowledge as bad as everything else they do? Could it be a good thing?

Philosophers are deeply interested in studying knowledge, what they call "epistemology." Philosophers ask seemingly silly questions like: "How do we learn things?" "Do I really know anything?" and "What is knowledge?" These questions will shed some light on the problem of the Magisterium. If we can come to understand what knowledge is and how it works, we can figure out whether the Magisterium should cover up the truth about certain important facts. As a matter of fact, we even may conclude that by hiding knowledge from inquiry, the Magisterium is actually helping to preserve knowledge!

The Magisterium has a lot of control over knowledge in Lyra's world. They determine what can be taught in schools and they can convict and execute anyone for heresy. So, many people in her world find themselves left in the dark. They only learn what the Magisterium wants them to learn. For example, Lee Scoresby points out, "Every philosophical research establishment, so he'd heard, had to include on its staff a representative of the Magisterium, to act as a censor and suppress the news of any heretical discoveries."[1]

It seems odd to even try to think of this as a good thing. We spend a great deal of time arguing that knowledge is power and that we should try to keep learning. Philosophers, especially, are motivated by learning and the pursuit of knowledge. For most of them, the pursuit of knowledge is the driving force of their lives. So how can the censorship of knowledge possibly be a good thing?

Descartes's Universe

To understand the argument that the Magisterium might use, we need a bit of a back story. We need to go all the way back to a philosopher named René Descartes and his work. In his book, *Meditations on First Philosophy,* Descartes tries to help us understand many things. His primary objective, though, is to provide a better account of knowledge. I say "better" because Descartes was very motivated to improve the way people in his time thought about knowledge.

Right before Descartes's birth, there had been some major changes in how people thought about the world. A couple of things violently shook the foundation of traditional knowledge: the earth was no longer considered to be the center of the universe by the scientific community and the Catholic Church's infallibility was challenged by Martin Luther. For our world this is like the people of Lyra's world learning that the Magisterium is wrong. Imagine being in her world and learning that the Authority is old and feeble, for example. Learning these things would shake the foundations of their society. Similarly, Descartes was born into a world in which recent unquestionable knowledge turn out to be wrong and dubitable.

This fact helped motivate Descartes to discover what should actually count as knowledge. If we can "know" something and then find out that it is wrong, it did not seem like that something should have been counted as knowledge in the first place. Descartes made

---

[1] Philip Pullman, *The Subtle Knife* (New York: Laurel-Leaf, 1997), p. 110.

it his goal to find something we could know for certain—indubitably. Descartes reasoning was that if a whole class of beliefs could be doubted, then those beliefs that fall into that classification should not be counted as knowledge. He believed that if we want to gain knowledge in those dubitable classes, that we must derive that knowledge from other, indubitable, truths. Descartes considers a series of classifications of beliefs like sensory knowledge and finds each class doubtable.

Descartes asks, "How do you know you are not dreaming?" as a way to doubt some of our most certain beliefs: when I am dreaming all of the laws of physics can appear very different from the way they are when I am awake. For some reason though, for the most part, I do not realize the fact that I am dreaming. Maybe we really live in Lyra's world and have dæmons of our own but we are only dreaming, right now, that we live in this more mundane world. Perhaps at any moment we will wake up and realize, much to our relief, that our dæmon is right there next to us and it was all just a bad dream. So how can I be certain that I am actually awake right now, and that the beliefs which depend on my being awake, like "I am reading a book right now," are correct?

Even the observable laws of physics may be doubted. Granted, it is pretty unlikely that I am dreaming right now. But, if you are dreaming right now you are very wrong about the fact that you are reading a book on *His Dark Materials.* You may argue in response to Descartes that there are things that cannot be questioned—like math. There is no question that two plus two, whether you are dreaming or not, can only equal four. There is no reasonable way we can doubt this. So maybe I can be certain that I know mathematical truths.

Descartes responds with an even weirder problem: what if we are being deceived? What if we are being deceived by some powerful dæmon or even by God himself? Perhaps, as in the world of *His Dark Materials,* God isn't perfect. Maybe, God actually enjoys messing with our heads. So we think that two plus two equals four, but in reality, two plus two equals five. Maybe we only think it equals four because this evil god is messing around with our thoughts and laughing all the while. Keep in mind that Descartes, at the end of his work, believed that we can have knowledge. He is not what philosophers call "a skeptic." Skeptics believe that we can't have knowledge because we can't be certain about anything. Descartes believed that we didn't have to worry about God deceiving us, for example, because an all-good god would not do that. Having said that, we might have more reason to worry that maybe God is like the Authority—too old and feeble to do much of anything and deceiving us about the real nature of the universe and our creation.

The Dubitable Nature of God and the Universe

Now, you may argue that these possibilities are very unlikely. Generally, philosophers refer to these unlikely possibilities as skeptical problems. As a matter of fact, we may have no reason to believe that we are dreaming or being deceived at all. On the other hand we have very good reason to believe that we are awake and that math is correct. As you are reading this, it seems as if all the evidence points to the fact that you are awake and that two plus two really does equal four and that you don't really live in Lyra's universe. But this doesn't mean that it's impossible for you to be dreaming or deceived right now, just really, really, *really,* unlikely.

This means that although we probably are right about the things we believe, we can't be sure. And this is all Descartes needs. It seems that that we cannot have knowledge if knowledge means that we are perfectly certain. It seems that that we cannot have knowledge if knowledge means that we are *sure.* We've been wrong in our beliefs before—the world is round though humanity claimed that it "knew" it was flat—matter is actually made of mostly empty space though we claimed we "knew" it was solid—and it might be that most of the world engages in conspiracy to deceive children on a regular yearly basis. It isn't likely that skeptical problems are legitimate, but they do end up being actual problems on occasion—on occasion we are wrong about the things that we believed to be true even though we claimed to "know" they are true.

Descartes does not let these skeptical problems—the fact that we may be dreaming or God is deceiving us, specifically—get in the way of his belief that he has knowledge. Descartes argues that although these seem like good skeptical problems at first, when we contemplate God we realize he would never deceive us. Unfortunately for philosophers today, we don't have that same certainty. Especially given the possibility that God may be decrepit and near death as he is in *His Dark Materials*; there's no reason to believe that God must be all-good and all-powerful. For example, it might be the case that we are right that there is a creator of the universe, but we might be wrong that that same creator is all-good. That creator may not care at all. Or, as in Lyra's world, we may come to realize that the being we think of as "The Authority" didn't even create the universe. We might learn, as Lyra did, that The Authority is actually feeble and is so old that it doesn't even run the universe. So, where Descartes was certain that he could know stuff because God was all-good, philosophers today cannot be quite that certain. God may be messing with our heads right now and everything we think we know is actually wrong.

Armored Bears Can Be Sure They Have Four Paws

So how do we deal with this skeptical problem? How can we say that we can know anything if we can't even be sure that we're awake right now? This seems like a silly question. Aren't I sure, for instance, that I have hands and that I am sitting at my computer using those hands to type? It just seems to go against common sense to worry about whether I'm actually dreaming right now. Well, if you think this is a good answer to the skeptic then you are in good company. G.E. Moore makes a common-sense argument, too. Moore's argument goes something like this: "the skeptic says we can't be sure we are awake and not dreaming, and, therefore, we can't be sure of anything else we think of as true. But the skeptic has it backwards! I know, for instance, that I have two hands, therefore, I know that I am not dreaming."[2] Moore thinks the fact that we can be so sure about our common-sense knowledge is evidence *against* the skeptic. So instead of worrying about whether or not I am actually here right now and not in bed asleep, I instead can assure myself that I am not dreaming or the victim of some grand illusion because of the knowledge that I have.

Not all skeptics buy Moore's argument, though. They think that he is playing unfairly. Moore may say something like "I know that I have two hands" but the obvious skeptical response is, "Well, how do you know that you are correct in saying that?" Maybe you're suffering from some horrible life-long coma state dream in which you *think* you have two hands, but, in fact, you really only

---

[2] G.E. Moore, "A Defense of Common Sense," *Philosophical Papers* (London, 1959).

have one? For Moore, this is just silly, because he believes that he knows he has two hands. But, is this really a silly concern or just a really *unlikely* concern? The fact is, it's unlikely that I'm dreaming right now or being deceived by a decrepit Authority. Nevertheless, that does not make it impossible. If Descartes is right, and I need to be *sure* in order to have knowledge, how can I say that I *know* that I have two hands? Moore thinks that fact that I know that I have two hands proves I am awake, but the skeptic thinks the fact that I don't know that I am awake proves I might be mistaken about having two hands. How fair is it, though, to simply say to the skeptic, "look I *know* I have two hands"? The skeptic wants us to give more reason to say we know something than just evidence that could be wrong, even if that evidence seems really good at the time.

Remember, for someone like Descartes, his reason for doubting common-sense things wasn't because he thought those common-sense things were wrong, but because *other common-sense beliefs have been wrong before.* We were wrong when we thought the world was flat. But if we went back in time to people, say five thousand years ago, who might have believed it was flat, they would have said it was just silly to think it was round. So, how can we tell the difference between those things which are common sense and are correct and things that are common sense that will be wrong in the future? Given how wrong we have been in the past, any one of our common-sense beliefs could turn out to be wrong with some ground breaking scientific revelation! It could turn out, for instance, that electrons actually have a kind of consciousness similar to Dust and so all matter has a kind of will to exist. But, let's be realistic for a moment, if we walk around all the time saying "maybe I'm dreaming," we are eventually going to make a big mistake. If in Lyra's world I walked up to an armored bear and kicked him and said "you might only be a dream, you can't hurt me!" I would quickly find myself mauled by a very angry, very big bear. So, it seems, something the skeptic is telling us must be wrong!

Why the Skeptics Have More to Prove than the Children

Fred Dretske thinks the skeptic is wrong and goes further than Moore to try to prove it. He thinks that it is not so much common-sense knowledge that proves we know things, but it's the fact that some skeptical problems are just not relevant to what we are talking about at all.[3] In other words imagine that you tell your friend you have just read *The Golden Compass* and she says in reply, "How do you know you actually read it? Maybe you dreamed that you read it." You might reply to her that you know by common sense that you read it, but that doesn't actually answer her question. Instead you can say "You're right, if I'm dreaming, then I did not read it, but it is up to *you* to prove to me that I am dreaming!" In other words, if I am talking about having read a book and someone starts talking to me about dreaming and that we might really just be asleep in Lyra's world they are bringing up something that has little or nothing to do with my statement, "I read *The Golden Compass.*" It seems that the skeptic's alternatives are irrelevant to the question at hand. Now if I say, 'Hmmmm, I wonder if I am dreaming" then the skeptic has very good reason to talk about dreaming. But, we only have to worry about dreaming or deceptive gods if they significantly connect to our claim. So I can know that I read the book, even though I don't know with hundred-percent certainty that I'm awake, because whether or not I am dreaming is irrelevant to the discussion I am having.

This answer to the skeptical problem is called the relevant alternatives approach. Philosophers like Dretske argue that we only need to worry about what the skeptic is saying if it is relevant to our knowledge claim. If you say you have read the book then you can know you've read it unless someone brings up a relevant problem like "but you can't read" or "the book doesn't exist." Then you can start worrying about whether you actually know you've read it or not. The idea is pretty easy; if I know that a skeptical argument is irrelevant to what I am saying, then I can know stuff. But, how do I know that the skeptical argument is irrelevant?

It seems, at first, very easy to say that you know an alternative is irrelevant. But, how do we know for sure? Of course it seems highly unlikely that I'm just dreaming about reading a book, but is it completely irrelevant, if I'm talking about knowledge? In other words, if I'm trying to figure out what I know and what I don't know, then the problem of dreaming is relevant. If a friend walks

---

[3] Fred Dretske, "Epistemic Operators," *The Journal of Philosophy* 67 (1970): 1007–1023.

up to me and says she has read a book, the problem of dreaming seems off topic, but if I am actually investigating what I know, then aren't the problems of dreams and dæmons very relevant?

Why Children Know More than Philosophers

So, now we are at a point where we complete the last leg of our journey towards the treatment of knowledge by the Magisterium. The philosopher David Lewis points out that, sometimes, skeptical questions are very relevant and sometimes they're completely irrelevant. He begins by pointing out that he knows all kinds of things. For example, I know that I am at a desk and I know that I am writing about a book, and I know that I have hands and so on. But, Lewis also recognizes that when I begin to examine these statements and ask myself, "do I really know these things?" certainty begins to dissolve. The deeper I investigate my knowledge claims, the less certain they become. So, yes, whilst these skeptical questions might not be a problem for everyday conversation, when we are actually trying to figure out what we know for sure, knowledge starts to slip away.

For obvious reasons Lewis's paper is titled "Elusive Knowledge." What he's really arguing is that epistemology—the examination of knowledge—destroys certainty. So it's not that I know nothing because of skeptical concerns; it's that when I investigate a knowledge claim it ceases to be certain. Lewis tells us that when we do epistemology we realize we can know very little. The deeper we dig the more possibilities appear which, though unlikely, results in less and less certainty. The actual act of examining knowledge produces more realizations of the ways we may be wrong.[4]

Think about it like this—you probably didn't consider the possibility that you are asleep until you decided to learn a little philosophy. Your own pursuit of knowledge has resulted in you having more reasons to doubt the very knowledge you gain. For example, Lyra didn't have much reason to doubt the Magisterium, *until she started asking questions about Dust.* Had she never done that she would have never had to deal with the problem of wondering whether she was being deceived.

---

[4] David Lewis, "Elusive Knowledge," *Australasian Journal of Philosophy* 74 (1996), pp. 549–567.

It seems that our level of certainty is dependent on context. Some philosophers argue for contextualism—they believe that we do get to have knowledge in certain contexts. Contextualists, like Dretske, argue against skepticism by pointing out that most of the time we can confidently say we know stuff because we aren't investigating knowledge itself. They recognize that the skeptic does present us with a problem when we're investigating knowledge, but normally we are not working in that context, normally we aren't investigating what it means to know stuff. Normally, in the context of everyday life, we are learning stuff and experiencing stuff and we get to say that we know that stuff. So, according to the contextualist, Lyra can say that she knows she's standing in the snow, for example. But, if she's investigating what it means to "know" stuff and tries to figure out if she "really" knows she is standing in the snow, then her context is different. Often, contextualists argue that this wondering what it means to "really" know is a bit silly when in most contexts it doesn't make sense to ask that question. Why should we go around asking "Do I really know this or really know that?"

Lewis is also arguing for contextualism, but he takes it to its logical conclusion. We can think of contextualists as maintaining that different contexts have different standards for what counts as knowledge. Most of the time the standards for what should count as knowledge are pretty low. But, when we question more deeply we start ratcheting up the standards. Yes, we can say that we know lots of things in most contexts, but when we're actually investigating knowledge itself we lose certainty and, thereby, we lose our claim to knowledge. Lewis's argument recognizes that if we completely ignore the question "Do I really know that?" then we also leave philosophy behind. Lewis points out that epistemology logically results in us asking deeper and deep questions about our knowledge claims—it raises the standards for knowledge significantly. So, in the context of philosophy, the question "how do I know that I know?" is a reasonable question to ask. But it may be one for which the standards are so high, in order to answer it, that we can never say that we actually know—we can never meet the standard.

We see this happen all the time. You might have even noticed this when reading *His Dark Materials*: those things that you were sure about before reading the books—like God is all good or there is only one universe—have become a good deal less certain because reading the books has resulted in you thinking more deeply. When you read the books and start thinking about the possibility that the world may be different than you initially thought, you start to engage in philosophy. It's when we actually inquire into things that we begin to see other perspectives and possibilities, and our certainty dissipates. For instance, you may believe that there is only one Earth and that parallel universes like Lyra's do not exist. As a matter of fact, if someone just randomly asked the question "How many Earths are there?" most people would *know* that the answer is "one." But, if the questioner pushes you to think hard about it and reflect on the possible other universes, you begin to become less certain. If you are honest and do not simply stamp your foot and yell "Because I know, darn it!" then your inquiry into the possibility of other earths that occupy the same metaphysical space as our own begins to become more real. You move from knowing, to not knowing *because of inquiry*.

This is ironic, of course, because generally when we think about knowledge we think that exploring and inquiring produces more knowledge. In actuality, though, inquiry produces doubt, more questions, and more inquiry. And that fact is the concern of the Magisterium. Consider this, *His Dark Materials* turns many traditional beliefs and knowledge claims upside down. The author forces us to explore the possibilities that God doesn't actually have some great grand plan, our mortal physical bodies are better than the spiritual, and those who rebel against God are good. In reading and thinking about Pullman's books, our certainty about God and the universe begins to waiver. But we would be poor philosophers if we walked away from the Magisterium saying "Well, they are very bad. Shame on them for trying to keep people ignorant" just because Pullman portrays them so horribly. With Lewis's argument in mind, let's dig a little deeper.

Is the Magisterium Trying to Save Knowledge or Just Trying to Destroy Inquiry?

What if the Magisterium realized what David Lewis realized? What if they realized that inquiry results in doubt. Lewis realized that if we mean "certainty" when we talk about knowledge, then knowledge is lost when we dig deeper because as we dig we learn more and more reasons to doubt what we learn. The Magisterium may think in a similar way. They may know that unquestioning belief is very important for the success of their plans. So, the may try to prevent inquiry because if the general populace starts digging they will lose certainty, and thereby the Magisterium's hope for the salvation of humanity will also be lost.

They believed they knew a few things that they thought were very important. As a matter of fact, they believed that these things were so important that certainty was necessary for happiness and peace. They might believe, for example, that if we start doubting those things—like doubting that God is all-powerful—then we cannot get into heaven. Well, then, doesn't it seem reasonable that they should try to prevent inquiry and thereby preserve certainty? They might have believed that as soon as the people of their world started asking probing questions, those people would doubt those things that the Magisterium *"knows" to be true!* And that doubt would lead to pain, suffering, and sin.

Well, the obvious question is then, "But wait! In the end wasn't the Magisterium wrong? Didn't it turn out that their ideas about God were mistaken? Wasn't all their effort to prevent others from learning about Dust a bad thing in the end?" Well, this is exactly the problem that Descartes started us with—how can we distinguish between those things that we know that are actually true and those things that just *seem true right now?* The great irony is that as soon as we start asking ourselves this question, everything we think we know becomes something that may turn out to be wrong in the future. It's unlikely, but possible. The Magisterium "knew" they were right, but it turned out they were wrong.

So, how do we judge the Magisterium? Should we praise them for trying to preserve knowledge or blame them for trying to prevent inquiry? For most philosophers the answer is going to be one that the Magisterium won't like. Lewis might be right, inquiry does destroy certainty—it results in higher standards for what we should count as knowledge. Unfortunately for the Magisterium questions like "Does God exist?" "Is God good?" and "What is Dust?" are all question that are deeply philosophical. In other words, answers to those questions must meet higher standards than normal. As a matter of fact the standards for philosophical questions are probably so high that we don't get to say that we "know" the answer; we only get to say that we "believe" we know the answer, for very good reasons, but we may be wrong. So obviously the Magisterium wants to avoid those questions in order to preserve certainty. But perhaps certainty just leads to intolerance and bigotry—like the Magisterium's—anyway.

Perhaps a little doubt is good. We may not get to know much when we are inquiring deeply, but that's ok because inquiry leads us to useful information, and doubt prevents thoughtless dogmatism. We can still learn when we inquire, gain understanding, and, perhaps, even gain a little wisdom at the expense of knowledge.

PART IV

Was There Only One World after All, which Spent Its Time Dreaming of Others?

11
Worlds of Possibility

HANNAH FINLEY

His Dark Materials is abundantly a story about worlds. From a myriad of alien settings, Philip Pullman draws such people and creatures as panserbjørne, Gallivespians, and mulefa. These worlds are normally inaccessible in the ordinary course of events, and in Lyra's homeworld they are known only to witches (who have, says Kaisa, "always known this," *Golden Compass*, p. 188) and a few cutting-edge Scholars, but at the conclusion of *The Golden Compass*, travel between these worlds becomes commonplace for the main characters. It can be accomplished by walking from one world to another via Lord Asriel's bridge, or by stepping through "windows" (either of no obvious origin, or cut open with the subtle knife Æsahættr). Angels have their own mechanism of travel, through a "form of seeing" mentioned by Xaphania (*Amber Spyglass*, p. 494).

Many of these worlds have clear commonalities. Lyra is unnerved by some of these in *The Subtle Knife*, "this Oxford was so disconcertingly different, with patches of poignant familiarity right next to the downright outlandish" (p. 74 and later). The Oxford she visits in Will's world bears obvious resemblance to the one she remembers from her own. From aspects of its broad layout, to the scratched initials of (at least in Lyra's version) Simon Parslow, she finds it familiar and is alarmed by the differences, including discarded chewing gum and the influence of automobiles.

It is strongly implied throughout the series that Will comes from "our world," and nothing about his home is any more unfamiliar to us than a non-fiction description of the real city would be. Therefore, the broad similarities between his world and Lyra's let us assume things about her world that are never explicitly stated.

There's every reason to suspect that Lyra's world has an island in the same place and of the same shape as our Madagascar, although it might go by another name; major figures in our ancient history likely appear in hers too; if you beat a bowl of cream for a long time in Lyra's world it will probably hold peaks and eventually turn into butter. Lyra herself meets with no suspicion when she visits Will's Oxford, indicating that she and her worldmates—apart from their dæmons—are normal humans.

Philosophers, too, like to talk about other worlds—these are actually a lot like the worlds in *His Dark Materials*, in that they are not physically obvious, commonly known about, or all just like our own. However, these philosophers' worlds are tools to talk about possibility (and are called "possible worlds" for that reason), not places to travel to and explore. Some philosophers have been known to hold that possible worlds really exist, "out there going on" (that phrase belongs to David Lewis, poster philosopher of possible world theory). Other theorists don't think that possible worlds exist in this way. To those more skeptical philosophers, possible worlds are just a convenient way to talk, in much the same way that it's commonplace to speak about fictional characters as though they really exist to avoid prefacing every sentence with "In the story . . ."

As far as the *His Dark Materials* series reveals, all of the worlds investigated have substantial parallelism. Even at a more fundamental level than the mirroring of twin Oxfords, and the presence of snakes in the world of the mulefa, we don't see (for instance) any otherworldly travelers who cannot breathe the same, customary sort of air, or who are crushed by the gravity of any setting they travel through. This could be a simple question of the books' scope. The scale of Asriel's army is immense and he demonstrates no baseless prejudice in favor of beings like himself, but he would find little benefit in recruiting (for instance) chlorine-breathers from a planet so low in mass that the pull of his alternate Earth would destroy them. And of course if Will tried to cut a window to a world whence such people might come, it would be suicide, chlorine being a poison to humans.

Still, if we assume that the worlds visited or mentioned in the story are an accurate representation of the variety of worlds that exist in *His Dark Materials*, possible worlds have them beat. They exclude only states of affairs that are *logically impossible*—which means that, to be ineligible for inclusion in *some* possible world, an event or object has to entail results that contradict one another. For example, square circles are logically impossible because the definitions of "square" and "circle" can't both apply to a single shape. All of the people, animals, objects, and events described in *His Dark Materials* are logically possible. In philosopher-speak, that translates to "there's at least one possible world in which each of these things exist." (And yes, that means that if you meet a philosopher who is what is called a "modal realist"—that is, the kind of philosopher who thinks possible worlds are really real, not just conventional tools—you may tease him or her about believing in talking bears.)

A World of My Own

In *His Dark Materials*, characters can and do leave their home worlds to explore, flee, recruit armies, or set loose all of the multiverse's ghosts so they can disintegrate and be reunited with the material realm. However, straying from one's origins for too long is hazardous: it causes deteriorating health and, eventually, death to spend more than a brief visit in an alien world. This weakened Will's father (although it didn't get a chance to kill him), and forced Will and Lyra to separate at the end of *The Amber Spyglass,* for if they did not, whichever one of them left home permanently would meet an untimely end. However, the effects can be alleviated by regular visits to the world of one's birth. This allowed Lord Carlo Boreal (a.k.a. Sir Charles Latrom) to live—apparently long-term—in Will's world, by making trips to his own (Lyra's) periodically. The explanation behind this is that the dæmons, visible like Lyra's or hidden like those of most other worlds, have a need for their native worlds or they sicken and die, taking their people with them.

In the case of possible worlds, going to a different one wouldn't do you (or your dæmon) any harm if the world was otherwise habitable, but on the other hand, you can't go to one in the first place. Travel between possible worlds is completely out of the question, even if you get hold of an atom-splitting knife. We live in a possible world—those philosophers who think possible worlds don't really exist only think that about *other* possible worlds, usually—and it gets a special title: "the actual world." Sometimes it's also called "alpha." And we are simply stuck here in alpha for all time; any world-traveling you might hope to do would just have to come in the form of going to visit *His Dark*

Materials-type worlds (if they exist here in the actual world), not other possible worlds.

In both cases, the world you're from has special properties, but with possible worlds, those properties are mostly linguistic. The actual world is the default "universe of discourse" that you "quantify over"—that's philosopher-speak for "what you're talking about when you say 'everything' or a word like it." Even a modal realist like David Lewis can say "talking bears don't exist" without lying or being mistaken. That's because even though modal realists are committed to saying that talking bears really inhabit other possible worlds, they don't believe there are any here in the actual world. Unless they specify otherwise, by using a word like "possibility" or "necessity" to serve as a clue that they're talking about other worlds too—it's assumed that they only mean the actual world.

The complicated part is that actuality is indexical—an indexical is a word that changes meaning depending on the circumstances in which it's used, like "me" or "here." So, in Lyra's possible world, if Lyra says "talking bears exist," it's true *because* of the assumption that she means her native possible world, not in spite of it. However, for reasons I'll discuss below, the words in *His Dark Materials* aren't as precise at picking out worlds as all that.

Tossing the Coin

In *The Golden Compass*, Lord Asriel explains to Lyra how other worlds come into being:

> Now that world, and every other universe, came about as a result of possibility. Take the example of tossing a coin: it can come down heads or tails, and we don't know before it lands which way it's going to fall. If it comes down heads, that means that the possibility of its coming down tails has collapsed. Until that moment the two possibilities were equal.
>
> But on another world, it does come down tails. And when that happens, the two worlds split apart. I'm using the example of tossing a coin to make it clearer. In fact, these possibility collapses happen at the level of elementary particles, but they happen in just the same way: one moment several things are possible, the next moment only one happens, and the rest don't exist. Except that other worlds have sprung into being, on which they *did* happen.

Mary Malone, a physicist, suspects that the worlds are "split off" from each other on the quantum level (*The Amber Spyglass*, p. 87).

If we consider her and Asriel to be reliable sources of information, then we know from whence the worlds in *His Dark Materials* come. Quantum indeterminacy on the level of the tiniest subatomic objects opens up several possible paths, and worlds multiply to go down each one, thereafter separate from one another. It's evident that over time these paths build up regularities in nature that are visible to the naked eye, like the dæmons.

Possible worlds have very different origin stories. To be precise, they don't come from anywhere at all. Things that are possible have *always* been possible and will always continue to be possible, because the laws of logic do not change and those laws are the only things that govern the limits of possible worlds. Therefore, all possible worlds can only exist eternally (unless there is such a thing as the "beginning of time", which is not uncontroversial).

A consequence of this is that *all* of the myriad worlds of *His Dark Materials* only take up *one* possible world. It is *possible* (logically) that random quantum events as Lord Asriel and Mary Malone describe could occur and cause dimensional splitoffs, and so those quantum events and resulting dimensional splitoffs happen in some possible world just as the books describe. For all their worldsliness (so to speak), Lyra, Will, and the other characters never get any farther away from their original possible world than you or I ever have.

But there is a catch. Remember David Lewis, the modal realist? He also had some ideas about the philosophy of fiction, specifically about what is called "underdetermination" by the text of stories. The *His Dark Materials* books do not *fully* describe a possible world. The books could expand to fill the entirety of Jordan College, both above and below ground, before they'd come close. Even if, instead of phrases like "lead-lined oak coffin," Pullman had said something like "a seven-foot-long, two-foot-deep, three-feet-wide-at-the-shoulders inch-thick coffin made from oak cut from such-and-such a forest by so-and-so the lumberjack on such-and-such a date and put together by so-and-so the coffinmaker and his apprentice who is also his son, lined with a three-millimeter layer of lead mined at . . ." he would not have fully described the world.

It would not be much of a work of fiction if the author had stopped in the middle of such an exciting story to list the names, dæmons, addresses, occupations, ages, and opinions on the flavor of marchpane for the entire population of Lyra's Oxford—let alone the much less relevant directory of the aforementioned alternate

Madagascar or a whole world that is never visited or mentioned. That's underdetermination: just about anybody could be living in those places, doing just about anything, without affecting the story put forth in the books at all! Even tinier details—the movement of motes of Dust, the timing down to the femtosecond of the flickering of the Northern Lights, the flapping of a butterfly dæmon's wings in Australia—are abundant and warrant, all by themselves, possible worlds to account for them.

So *His Dark Materials* describes not just a single possible world, but many—an incredibly vast number of fully complete worlds, some radically different in some aspects that are just locally unimportant to the story. In every one of them, the action of the tale unfolds just as described—the worlds differ in things like the composition of the population of Madagascar, or the thread count of coal-silk garments, or the exact number of hairs in Pantalaimon's coat when he settles in his pine marten shape, or other details that did not bear mentioning. It's possible for these things to have come out almost any which way, so there's a world to account for all of their possibilities in every possible combination.

Still, each possible Lyra going through the adventures in the books stays to her own possible world, never straying from it. There is no danger of Lyra-1 going through a window and finding herself in Cittàgazze-2 or Will's-Oxford-9,347, even if she would never notice. Mary-1 can visit mulefa-1 such that a zaril who died six years prior to her visit was killed by a falling seedpod while Mary-2 visits mulefa-2 such that the same zaril was the victim of the same seedpod, which just had a bug on it at the time it fell; just because this makes no difference to either Mary does not mean that they are metaphysically interchangeable.

"Perhaps There Was a Lyra"

In *The Subtle Knife*, Lyra is unsettled by how similar and yet different her Oxford and the one in Will's world that she's exploring are. She notices the initials SP, indiscernible from the ones carved by Simon Parslow in her home city, and reflects, "There might be a Simon Parslow in this world. Perhaps there was a Lyra." She never meets an otherworldly Lyra—or any other person whose alternate version she's already encountered, for that matter—but it still brings up a field of theorizing that gets a lot of attention in the realm of possible worlds as well.

Surely, goes the reasoning, it is possible that some real person—Philip Pullman, for instance—could have had something different happen to him or her. Pullman could have written four books in the *His Dark Materials* series instead of three. That means that there is some possible world in which there lives someone almost exactly like the actual world's Pullman, except that in this other world, the fellow published a book called, perhaps, *The Intention Craft*. But it is a truth about the actual Philip Pullman that he never published a novel entitled *The Intention Craft*. So how can it be that our alpha-world-Pullman is the same person? Isn't it *possible that* (and therefore the case in a possible world that) alpha-Pullman could have written *The Intention Craft*?

One way to explain this awkwardness is with what's called the "counterpart relation," which describes the relationship for one person or object and another one that the first could have been. The man in a nearby possible world who wrote *The Intention Craft* isn't alpha-Pullman, but he *is* someone related to alpha-Pullman as a counterpart by virtue of being very similar to him in most ways (except in those respects that must be different to allow the publication of the counterpart's extra novel). The counterpart relation is mutual, so from the perspective of the author of *The Intention Craft*, alpha-Pullman is a counterpart of his, who represents the possibility that *His Dark Materials* could have been only three books long (plus a few supplementary novellas).

In spite of the way that worlds split off from each other in *His Dark Materials*, the potential other Lyra that the protagonist finds so unsettling could still be her counterpart. Some philosophers have maintained that worldmates (inhabitants of the same possible world, not HDM-style world) can also bear the counterpart relation to each other. For example, if you're similar enough to Philip Pullman that you could have been him, then you and he bear the counterpart relation to one another. Lyra could, similarly, bear the counterpart relation to someone very like her from Will's world.

Lyra is also, of course, a counterpart to individuals from other possible worlds. I mentioned that there exists a vast array of possible worlds in which the events of *His Dark Materials* take place—each of them has a Lyra, all of whom are assuredly counterparts to one another. Perhaps the Lyra who should have worried our heroine by her possibility was not the one who might have been born in Will's world to begin with, but the one who might have been moving through an indistinguishable Oxford, an indiscernible

Pantalaimon in her pocket, thinking the same thoughts and feeling the same worries, and separated only by the presence or absence of an extra mote of Dust in a place she'd never visit or hear of. (For if it is possible that the mote of Dust be there and possible that it not exist, then there must be possible worlds in which each is the case.)

12

Lyra's Journey to the World of the Dead

ANGELA RHYAN HARRIS and PAUL BAER

LYRA: But he [Pan] *is* me!
THE BOATMAN: If you come, he must stay.
LYRA: But we can't! We'd die! —

—*The Amber Spyglass*

What does Lyra mean when she says "Pan *is* me"? Does she mean that Pantalaimon is a part of her? Or is she asserting that she and Pantalaimon are literally one and the same person? Lyra's claim illustrates the ambiguity surrounding the concepts of 'sameness' and 'identity': whether something counts as the same thing. In order to figure out how to interpret Lyra's claims, we need more information.

How can we decide whether *this* is the same person as *that*?

- **Are you the same person you were yesterday, or twenty years ago? If so, why?**

- **If a human body appears to be inhabited by several different personalities, are there several persons or only one? Can one of them commit murder while the others remain innocent?**

- **If a human is in a long-term coma, is it a person, and if so, is this the same person who owned that body before the coma?**

- **If a person has a head injury which gives them total amnesia for most of what they knew before the injury,**

153

so that they cannot recall anyone they knew, are they the same person they were?

- **In a case of conjoined twins, where there is one body, is there one person or two?**

These are just a few of the puzzles of personal identity. At first it might seem child's play to answer such questions, but as we pursue them, we find more and more puzzles.

The "Soul" Criterion for Personal Identity

In their conversation about making the frightening life-or-death decision to journey to the world of the dead, Lyra and Will want to know whether or not they will be able to return if they make a trip to the world of the dead—whether they will survive—and if so, how? Lyra consults her alethiometer to find out if the world of the dead is a place they can get to using Will's knife. The alethiometer confirms that in fact they can get to the world of the dead, but it's a strange place from which they may never return.

> Will, . . . [the world of the dead is] So strange . . . Could we really do that? Could we really go to the land of the dead? But—what part of us does that? Because dæmons fade away when we die—I've seen them—and our bodies, well, they just stay in the grave and decay, don't they?
>
> Then there must be a third part. A different part. You know . . . I think that must be true! Because I can think about my body and I can think about my dæmon—so there must be another part, to do the thinking!
>
> Yes. And that's the ghost. (*The Amber Spyglass*, p. 166)

If Lyra's conclusion is true, then humans have parts: the body, the dæmon, and the thinking part. In this case, survival is possible for those kinds of things who have the essential characteristic of being a thinking thing in the form of a ghost. It's this kind of reasoning in Descartes's *Meditations* that leads to his famous views on mind-body distinctness.

If your ghost is essential to your persisting, what is it about your ghost that would make it count as the kind of thing we could rightfully call "you"? Particular problems are raised if we take souls or ghosts as non-physical substances. For example, how does a physical thing transfer information like experiences and memories, also currently taken to be physical, onto an immaterial substance?

Another problem is that it makes no sense to locate an immaterial substance in space or time, so how do we explain its location in your body? Inability to respond adequately to these problems isn't necessarily fatal for the same soul criterion for identity. But at this point we are pressed to explain the reasons for considering it as a candidate for the identity of any person; after all, God may be the only being who could recognize our soul.

The Same-Body Criterion for Personal Identity

In contrast, let's consider the same-body criterion for personal identity. It's having a unique body that makes us who we are, and having the same body that allows us to survive.

In *The Amber Spyglass*, Will and Lyra seek out Iorek, the armored bear, who has the skills required to mend the knife they need to journey to the world of the dead. Iorek agrees to mend the knife but warns the children of the risks:

>]If you do not find a way out of the world of the dead, we shall not meet again, because I have no ghost. My body will remain on the earth, and then become a part of it. But if it turns out that you and I both survive, then you will always be a welcome and honored visitor to Svalbard. (*The Amber Spyglass*, p. 196)

If Iorek is right, then armored bears do not survive death, and the necessary condition for the persistence of armored bears is having the same body.

On the face of it, the same body seems like a perfectly reasonable criterion. It's certainly in line with contemporary science. Having the same body is one of the primary ways others are able to identify us over time. However, a consequence of this view is that you are identical with your decomposing corpse. The amount of decomposition that can occur before your corpse is no longer the same person remains an open question. A non-arbitrary line must be drawn somewhere between a newly dead body and a dispersed group of atoms, such that on one side it's still the same person as you and on the other it is not. It turns out to be incredibly difficult to draw such a line.

Nonetheless, reasons are available to argue for the importance of bodies in practical questions. Consider the respect demanded in the treatment of bodies in persistent vegetative states, or when it comes to rituals and rights concerning the bodies of the dead. It really does matter to us that it's not just any dead body; imagine going to a loved one's funeral expecting to see their face one last time and just when you get to the casket you are shocked to see that the dead body in the casket is someone else. While it seems the same-body criterion won't help us with surviving death, it might nevertheless be a necessary condition for the identity of a person over time. The particularly important benefit associated with the same-body view is that it provides persistence conditions for a broader class of individuals we are inclined to treat as having moral worth, such as newly born infants and those who are in a persistent vegetative state.

The Same-Psychology Criterion for Personal Identity

The dæmon changed again. He did so in the flick of an eye, and from a goldfinch he became a rat, a powerful pitch-black rat with red eyes. (*The Subtle Knife*, p. 25)

The ability to change shape instantaneously is a skill with a long history, from the Greek gods to Mystique in the X-men. So it's not at all surprising to us—in fiction anyway—that a being could remain the same "person" in different forms. We generally have no doubt in such circumstances that whatever is fundamental has remained the same in spite of the shift.

What is it that stays the same through the change? It's hard to put it simply, but it's most intuitive that it's something psychological. We could go back to Lyra's "part to do the thinking," or, similarly, to Descartes's. But whereas Descartes believed in an immaterial soul, it was the great British philosopher John Locke who identified the "self"—the basis of personhood in moral terms—explicitly in consciousness, and in the continuity of psychological phenomena like memory. Indeed, while it is a bit of an oversimplification, Locke's view is often referred to as "the memory criterion."

Locke uses thought experiments in order to get rid of the confusion surrounding the question of personal identity in essence and in regard to moral questions. His examples are used to show that, through reflection upon the way in which we think about our "self," we can see that the essence of a person does not necessarily consist in the same substance, material or immaterial, nor in the same human animal, but in consciousness. In a short but famous example, Locke writes in his *Essay Concerning Human Understanding*:

> . . . should the Soul of a Prince, carrying with it the consciousness of the Prince's past Life, enter and inform the Body of a Cobbler as soon as deserted by his own Soul, everyone sees, he would be the same Person with the Prince, accountable only for the Prince's Actions. . . .

Leaving aside here the use of "Soul," it's the emphasis on consciousness and memory that is important:

> 'Tis plain consciousness, as far as ever it can be extended, should it be to Ages past, unites Existences, and Actions, very remote in time, to the same Person, as well as it does the Existence and Actions of the immediately preceding moment: So that whatever has the consciousness of present and past Actions is the same Person to whom they both belong.

Plainly, part of our intuition that Pan is the same whether finch or rat, ermine, dog, or dolphin, is that his consciousness has memories of his experiences in all previous forms. Similarly, we assume that with dæmons (or other beings) that change shape, it is their consciousness—their 'personality'—that allows others to identify them as the same dæmon.

Derek Parfit is a contemporary philosopher who is credited for expanding on, and arguably improving, Locke's memory criterion of personal identity. In Parfit's account of what's rational for a person to be concerned with when anticipating the future, Parfit offers a more robust account of what's important to us in terms of the way in which we think of ourselves, which includes things like beliefs, desires, goals, and egoistic concerns about one's future.

Parfit also rejects identity as the person-preserving relation and argues that what we really care about when it comes to our future is whether or not we survive. Survival requires what Parfit calls psychological connectedness and continuity (PCC). While a precise definition is difficult, psychological continuity involves the maintenance of our psychological features over time—not just memories, but intentions, beliefs, desires and values (examples of what Parfit calls "psychological connections").

Parfit argues that psychological continuity and survival can be partial, and can even have a "one-to-many" relationship. This latter claim resolves a paradox in "splitting" cases—if each half of my brain, with my consciousness on-board, is put in a new body, my old self appears to be identical to each future self, but they are not identical to each other. This violates the transitivity condition of identity (if a is identical to b and b to c, then a is identical to c). If we dispense with concerns about identity *per se*, we can simply say that my consciousness has survived as two now-separate consciousnesses, which will have the same memories and other psychological features initially but which will diverge over time.

One apparent advantage of Parfit's view is that it can accommodate intuitions we have about cases where breaks in memory occur, such as severe amnesia or brain damage cases. Parfit's rejection of identity ironically results in the claim that is irrational to have concern for our future self; since our future self exists only in imagination, we have no PCC with it. This raises a difficulty for Parfit in explaining the rationality of self-improvement, because it relies on the assumption of identity, followed by the assumption, *contra* Parfit, that it is rational to be concerned with what happens to ourselves in the future.

Hester in the Sky with Diamonds

When the ghosts are freed from the world of the dead, they become sets of conscious atoms, and the example of Lee and Hester shows that the dæmons do wait for their humans, though the dæmons are also in the form of conscious atoms, and their humans (when things go as they are meant to) return to their dæmons in the form of atoms. We also learn that all the particles in the universe are conscious at some level:

> . . . the last little scrap of the consciousness that had been the aeronaut Lee Scoresby floated upward . . . conscious only of his movement upward, the last of Lee Scoresby passed through the heavy clouds and came out under the brilliant stars, where the atoms of his beloved dæmon, Hester, were waiting for him. (*The Amber Spyglass,* p. 418)

What should we say about Lee and Hester? Should we count this as a case of genuine survival, in which enough of the important features of a person (or human-dæmon) are maintained? If so, then, in cases where all matter is conscious, it looks like neither the body, in its standard form, nor the ghost is necessary or sufficient conditions for survival.[1] The same soul criterion can only say they survive if we include the proviso that souls can continue in the form of conscious material particles. However, this is problematic because it lacks evidence, it's not the traditional version of the soul and is therefore *ad hoc*, and if we add the proviso, then the soul doesn't add any explanatory power. These problems don't rule out the possibility of the same-soul criterion, but it then puts the burden of explanation on the advocate of that view. The same-body criterion is ruled out as it doesn't require consciousness and we no longer have a body. It seems then that a same-psychology criterion might be the best account to accommodate what happens here as a successful case of survival.

Locke's same-consciousness account may be the one best suited to accommodate persons in *His Dark Materials* particularly because Locke places no constraints on the kind of substance required for the location of unified consciousness. Parfit's PCC account may be an alternative to Locke's, although one problem for Parfit is posed by the time the dæmon atoms are separated from the atoms which constitute their human part, which is in ghost form and stuck in the world of the dead until freed. Why isn't the break in psychological connectedness and continuity enough to cause a failure of survival? Both Locke's and Parfit's views are under strain because of the complexity of humans with dæmons, their deep connection to each other causing them to have the same existence conditions, in the sense that if one's body dies, the other's does too. We're still left with the question of whether they survive in cases in which humans become ghosts and dæmons become bits of conscious matter.

A contemporary view that might address this is the matter criterion, which says wherever there is a material object it is identical to a specific quantity (hunk) of material bits. An ice cube is identical to the number of water molecules in that particular ice cube. On this view, we take people as a kind of object; a person, according to this view is identical to the number the small material bits (atoms), in

---

[1] See David Chalmers's *The Conscious Mind* for a contemporary defense of the possibility that all matter is conscious.

that particular person. In the worlds of HDM it turns out that everything is made up of conscious atoms. This is a version of the same matter view, called panpsychism, which says you are identical to the number of conscious bits of material that make you up.

Let's vary the example to see if our intuitions change about survival when we use ordinary humans. Suppose you learn that a meteor is going to hit the Earth tomorrow shattering it to pieces. Nothing on the planet will survive. However, you have the good fortune of having a very creative friend who has built a matter-transformation machine which will cause you to change from your current embodied form to a group of tiny bits of conscious atoms— the very same bits that make you up currently—at which time they will float up into the atmosphere together, just like Lee Scoresby, and allow you to escape the Earth's destruction. Would you risk the transformation to avoid certain destruction? And if so, do you think you would be the same person in the way that matters most?

Individuation: Am I One or Are We Two?

Consider where we began—where Lyra declares that "Pan is me." In her very next line she declares that "*we* would die." And indeed, we know that humans and dæmons share a physical bond that can be cut with a physical knife, and that indeed if one dies, the other dies also. But we also know that they do not share all aspects of their consciousness, and that one can act independently of the other. So: are they one object or two? One person or two?

This raises the problem called "individuation"—distinguishing individual things from other things. These questions are relevant in our own world as well. We can also ask if the "object" created by the sharing of parts, creating a bond between what looks more or less like two bodies, should be considered a single individual or two. Does the answer depend on how many of the parts overlap? And does it change if there is only one "consciousness" or two? Answers to these questions can help guide us in cases of conjoined twins, as well as so-called "split brain" cases.

Personal Identity and Moral Questions: Who Cares?

Many other practical and moral questions provide motivation for enquiry into personal identity, but we'll only briefly glance at two kinds that rely heavily on answering the questions about individuation and require sameness of a person over time: our conception that *reward and punishment* demand that they go to the same person who committed the act, and *contractual obligations*, which also call for the conditions to apply only to the same person who set up the contract.

Difficult complications arise in multiple personality disorder (MPD) cases of punishment, and of persons in a persistent vegetative state (PVS) and their living will.

Multiple personality disorder, put simply, is a psychological condition in which more than one "personality" seemingly resides in the same body. There's no consensus among psychiatrists and psychologists as to whether it's a genuine condition or an incorrect description of something else. Let's grant for now that it does occur in some cases.

Consider the following case (based loosely on the movie *Primal Fear*) as if it were presented in a court and you are a jury member. A murder has occurred and the alleged killer has been located and is now on trial. A complication arises if the alleged killer suffers from MPD. Suppose for the sake of argument that we're in Texas where punishment for murder is the death penalty; MPD is an undisputed disorder. The defendant, call him "Ted," is called to the witness stand where he timidly describes what happened. "I witnessed the murder and was terrified. I wanted to do something to prevent it, but I couldn't move." Ted's account gets only some of the details right while others are simply unavailable to him. The clever prosecutor does something during cross-examination which successfully provokes and "brings out" the dominant personality, call him Ed. Ed proudly owns up to the murder and is able to give precise details of what happened, some of which could not have been known to anyone but the murderer and the investigating officer. At this point it is up to you to decide the fate of Ted, Ed, and however many other personalities reside in the body.

Can any of our candidates for essential characteristic criteria for identity help us in answering the individuation question, which we will call the counting question (the question regarding the number of individuals that are present)?

> **Soul:** On the view that claims the soul is essential, it's not obvious what it might contribute to the counting question. There is nothing that defines whether each personality has a soul,

or more than one soul. One soul could also have multiple personalities.

BODY: On the view that the body is essential, the answer is obvious. In the MPD case it's clear that there is only one body. It's a bit trickier when dealing with humans with dæmons, or with conjoined twins; in both of these examples, a case can be made that there is only one body or that there are two bodies bound together.

PSYCHOLOGY: The view that we are essentially our psychology, broadly construed, seems to suggest that the number of personalities gives us the answer to the counting question: three personalities, three individuals. But if we go by the memory criterion then it depends on what the different personalities can remember. On the psychological connectedness view, the answer depends on how close the overlapping chains of psychological connections are between the personalities. If three are sufficiently closely connected then the answer would be one. Alternatively, if there were few or zero psychological connections between personalities, then again the number of personalities gives us the answer, keeping in mind that Parfit admits of degree.

CONSCIOUS MATTER: If we are essentially the total sum of the conscious atoms that constitute us, the answer to the counting question seems to be one, though we as an object will look quite strange if we include all of the atoms that have ever been a part of us some will be spread out.

Does the answer you arrive at affect your judgment on punishment? Now, consider that you are not a member of the jury, but rather, Ted, the "witness" personality—would this affect your answer?

A similar case can easily be imagined in the world of *His Dark Materials*. We know that Pan can act against Lyra's will, as evidenced by his affection towards Will, in violation of the rules of their society. Suppose instead that Pan had killed somebody. Would Lyra also be guilty? If for some reason Pan's murder were punishable by death, which would also kill Lyra, would this seem to be just?

Another set of practical concerns that involve personal identity arise from questions about the enforcement of contracts. Plainly a contract is intended to bind the same persons who signed it (leaving aside matters of inheritance), and usually this is not an issue. However, this is not always true. Consider the matter of a person in a persistent vegetative state (PVS)—a long-term coma. If such a person left a living will addressing, for example, their desire to be kept alive (or not) on life-support machinery, it's precisely in such a situation (being in a PVS) that it is supposed to apply. But it's not obvious that the person in the PVS is, on all accounts, the same person that wrote the living will.

13

Why the Dead Choose Death

RICHARD GREENE

Lots of people die in Philip Pullman's *His Dark Materials* trilogy. In fact lots of creatures both natural and supernatural, including God (aka The Authority) die throughout the work.

Lee Scoresby is shot to death (his corpse is eaten by his panser-bjørne friend Iorek Byrnison), the powerful angel Metatron, along with Lord Asriel and Mrs. Coulter fall to their deaths into an abyss, and Iofur Raknison is killed in hand-to-hand (or, rather, paw to paw) combat with Iorek Byrnison, just to name a few. Much like our real—non-fictional—world a lot is made of death. It's to be avoided, it's considered to be tragic, it's something to be mourned, the death of one individual can greatly affect the lives of billions of others (in ways both positive and negative), and dying can be quite unpleasant, though it need not be.

These facts about death (along with a handful of others) raise a number of compelling philosophical questions about the nature of death and the purported badness of death: What is it to be dead? What constitutes death? Is death permanent? Can one survive one's own death? What makes death bad? And so forth. Pullman's *His Dark Materials* addresses some of these questions and turns others on their ears.

The Puzzling Nature of Death

The epicurean philosophers of ancient times held, oddly enough, that death couldn't be a bad thing. They thought that as long as one existed, then death wasn't present (at least not the death of the individual in question). Once someone died, then they didn't exist anymore, so there was never any death-related badness for that person. This view was based on a couple of assumptions: (1) that upon death one ceased to exist, so death doesn't involve something like an afterlife, and (2) in order for something to be bad for an individual, that person would have to somehow "experience" the badness. The epicurean view, therefore, raises a puzzle about death. How can death be bad, if one isn't around to experience the badness?

Subsequent philosophers have raised a second puzzle about the badness of death, which is sometimes called "the asymmetry puzzle." The idea behind this puzzle is that the time before a person is born is not regarded as a bad thing, but the time after one dies is regarded negatively, even though, metaphysically speaking, both times are identical—at each time one does not exist. Why should one period of non-existence be regarded negatively while another is regarded neutrally or with indifference?

Of course each of these puzzles could easily be resolved by taking the position that death is not bad. This, however, doesn't quite jibe with most people's intuitions about death, and it certainly doesn't jibe with people's behaviors. People typically will go to great lengths to avoid death, including very religious people, who believe that upon death their lot will be greatly improved. Referring to the Pope driving around in his bullet-proof pope-mobile, Drew Carey quipped, "If that guy is afraid to die, then I'm really in trouble."

The various characters in *His Dark Materials* adopt pretty much the same attitudes with respect to death as do folks in the real world. In the very first pages of the trilogy our heroine, Lyra Belacqua, acts to prevent the murder of her "uncle," Lord Asriel. Will Parry's journey begins as he acts to save his feeble mother from sinister men looking for letters from her long lost husband, John Parry, whom he believes pose a danger to his mother's life. Later Will grieves the death of his father at the hands of Juta Kamainen, a witch whose advances John Parry once spurned. The Gallivespians, two thumb-sized spies who travel on the backs of dragon flies, frequently leverage their position by wielding deadly poisonous spurs. As regards death, even the moral attitudes of the characters in *His Dark Materials* parallel our own. For example, Father Gomez, a priest in service of The Authority feels the need to seek a preemptive absolution, which is a sort of pre-forgiveness, before setting out to murder Lyra (it was prophesized that Lyra's heroic journey would result in the end of The Authority's reign).

The similarities between Pullman's world and our own signal that the aforementioned simple response to our puzzles about death is likely not going to be applicable to the characters in *His Dark Materials*, either. Their attitudes and actions simply don't bear out that for them death is not a bad thing.

The Badness of Death

So just what is so bad about death? This question, as we've seen can't be answered by appealing to what death seems or feels like, because death isn't experienced. Many theorists endorse some version of what has come to be known as the "Deprivation View," which is the view that the badness of death lies in its depriving persons of the good things that life has to offer (if one is dead, one can't enjoy things such as Zeppelin rides or racing across rooftops). Notice that the Deprivation View doesn't account for the badness of death by making reference to things experienced; rather, it cashes out the badness of death in terms of things not experienced. To illustrate, suppose that Father Gomez had been successful in his attempt to assassinate Lyra. Lyra would have missed out on almost the entirety of what promises to be a full and wonderful life. Lyra's future has her studying with the scholars at the Oxford of her world. She will learn to master reading the alethiometer. She will enjoy deep personal relationships, she will travel, and so forth. As long as Lyra's future has more good in it than bad, the Deprivation View renders the judgment that Lyra's death is a bad thing. This will be true for anyone whose future is worth living: their death will be a bad thing in virtue of the future goodness of which they are deprived by death.

Another plausible view of the badness of death that doesn't account for the badness of death by making reference to things experienced is the Desire Frustration View. Advocates of this view hold that death is bad because it signals the frustration of desires; desire frustration is generally taken to be a bad thing, although it is certainly true that having certain desires frustrated is probably good (for example, it would appear to be a very good thing were my desire to inject heroin to be frustrated). Suppose that Iofur Raknison had been victorious in his battle to the death with Iorek Byrnison. Since Iorek had a number of significant desires, such as regaining his position among the panserbjørne, serving as the ruler of the panserbjørne, and helping Lyra on her quest, to the extent that his desires would have been frustrated by his death, his death it appears would have been a bad thing.

I'm not going to attempt to adjudicate the debate over which of these views (if either) is the correct view of the badness of death. Both look promising, each provides a response to our two puzzles about the badness of death, and each *seemingly* applies equally well to Pullman's worlds as they do to our world.

Death in the Worlds of *His Dark Materials*

So what exactly happens when a person dies in the worlds of *His Dark Materials*? At first glance it appears pretty similar to death in our world—bodies go limp or explode or burn (depending on the circumstances of the death), and all signs of life vanish. There is one important difference: in those of Pullman's worlds, such as Lyra's world, in which persons have dæmons, the dæmon can be seen to vanish at the precise moment of death.[1]

There are a couple of things worth noting about this difference. First, it points to a sort of dualism, at least for human beings, in Pullman's worlds (the panserbjørne, for example, don't have dæmons): humans have a physical body and a soul of sorts, which roughly manifests itself as a dæmon. This is a non-standard dualism, as the dæmon is also physical, in nature, but this is not of great concern for our purposes. Second, there's nothing about this difference (the addition of a vanishing dæmon upon death) to raise a problem for either the Deprivation View or the Desire Frustration View of the badness of death as being applicable to Pullman's worlds. In fact, it lends some support to the claim that these views get things right in those worlds in which persons have dæmons.

The assumption that proponents of the various accounts of the badness of death make is that death is an "experiential blank." Recall the epicurean puzzle: when one is dead one has no experiences. A common reaction to the literature on the badness of death involves raising the possibility of an afterlife. What if death is really good? What if one goes to heaven when one dies? Stories involv-

---

[1] There's a healthy debate going on in both philosophical and medical communities as to whether a whole-brain or a higher-brain criterion should be employed when determinations of death are made. The occurrence of a vanishing dæmon would go a long way toward resolving a number of the issues surrounding determination of death.

ing an afterlife typically involve explaining how a part of us survives death—the body dies, but the spirit or soul or mind lives on. Well, if the physical body dies and the soul dies (that is, the dæmon dies), then there's nothing left to survive one's death, and stories of an afterlife don't factor in to the discussion of death's badness.

The World of the Dead

The accounts of the badness of death we've been considering have fared well thus far. Unfortunately, matters are not quite as simple as they first appear. In *The Amber Spyglass*, the third installment in *His Dark Materials*, Lyra and Will decide to venture into the world of the dead in order to make contact with Lyra's friend Roger and Will's father.

Upon entering the "suburb of the dead"—a dreary "shanty town" just across the river from the world of the dead, Lyra and Will discover that each person has a ghost that survives his or her death and has what is called a "death." One's death is a shadowy figure that comes into existence when one is born, sticks around unnoticed throughout one's life, and at the moment of death taps one on the shoulder and escorts one across the river and into the world of the dead.

So there is at least one thing that survives one's dying: one's ghost (one's death also survives, but it is not clear whether one's death is a part of it or just something assigned to one at birth). This means that the situation regarding the badness of death in Pullman's worlds is a bit more complicated that it initially seemed. In addition to one's physical body and one's dæmon, one has a ghost. Perhaps one's dæmon is not one's soul after all, but rather, the place where the soul is housed during one's life. Perhaps, alternatively, the soul is itself not a simple thing, which partially inhabits one's ghost and partially inhabits one's dæmon (Plato held that the soul actually had three parts: the reasoning part, the spirited part, and the appetitive part). The text is not entirely clear on this matter. At any rate, it's not obvious that either the Deprivation View or the Desire Frustration View will be able to account for the badness of death or for that matter it is not, at this point in the discussion, clear whether death is even a bad thing in Pullman's worlds. It all depends, of course, on what lies across the river.

Upon attempting to cross the river into the world of the dead, Lyra is informed by the Boatman—a character strongly reminiscent of Charon the boatman from ancient Greek mythology who would ferry the dead across the river Styx and into the underworld—that her dæmon will not be allowed to accompany her on the voyage. Lyra reports a sensation of her dæmon, Pan, being ripped from her heart. Will and the Gallivespians report experiencing a similar sensation, even though they don't themselves have dæmons (presumably it is their souls that are being left behind, but again, it's not entirely clear). Upon reaching the world of the dead Lyra and her party are attacked by harpies. Ghosts inform the group that the world of the dead is a miserable place where nothing ever happens except torment by harpies. The harpies cause hopelessness and despair in the ghosts by constantly reminding them of bad things about themselves and their lives.

So this seems sufficient to account for the badness of death in Pullman's worlds. The afterlife is full of bleakness and periods of boredom, which are only broken up by despair inducing torment at the hands of the harpies. Moreover, the pain that Lyra felt upon becoming separated from Pan is perpetual and not limited to those persons that have a dæmon. Recall that Will and the Gallivespians felt the same sensation as Lyra. It turns out that any creature with a soul will, upon entering the land of the dead, become separated from their soul and experience the same misery.

So death *is* a horrible experience after all in the worlds of *His Dark Materials*. The Deprivation View and the Desire Frustration View are unnecessary, in that they were employed to explain how death can be bad given that death is an experiential blank. Moreover, to the extent that the dead are still deprived of the good things in life and their desires are still frustrated, those facts appear to be far outweighed by the sheer misery of spending eternity in the world of the dead, being tortured by harpies, and experiencing a painful separation from one's soul (or dæmon, as the case may be).

Why the Dead Choose Death

While it appears that we've accounted for the badness of death in Pullman's worlds, we've not yet answered the central question of this chapter: why do the dead choose death. That's because our story still contains a twist or two.

As it turns out, the afterlife is not exactly death. People's bodies have died, and their dæmons have vanished into thin air (in the film version of the *The Golden Compass* dæmons appear to explode upon death), and all that remains is a sort of ghostly existence, but there is one final step that the dead might possibly take.

Will and Lyra desire to help the dead. They negotiate with the harpies to stop tormenting the ghosts in exchange for the ghosts regaling the harpies with interesting stories from their lives, but this is not enough—Will and Lyra want to release the dead from the world of the dead (even without the harpies' torment, there is still the pain of being separated from one's dæmon and the day to day boredom of being in the world of the dead). They accomplish this by using Will's knife (the titular "subtle knife") to cut a hole into another world. The dead (well, most of them anyway) flee the world of the dead without hesitation. As they enter the new world they vanish in a fashion similar to dæmons upon "death." At this point their atoms link up with their dæmons' atoms and they join the universe. The resulting state is nirvana-esque.

So now we have the answer to our question. The dead choose death because it is better than the afterlife. Again, the afterlife is mind numbingly dull and full of despair. Death is, at minimum, neutral, with some possibility of being a positive experience, since the dead ultimately become Dust, which is the basis for conscious experience. Again, the text is a little unclear on such details. At any rate, on any utilitarian calculus death is a preferable state of affairs to the afterlife. At the point in which death is an option, the afterlife is the only other option.

Does this mean that since the afterlife is distinct from death in Pullman's worlds, the Deprivation View and the Desire Frustration View are back on the table? Recall that they only failed to account for the badness of death when the afterlife was actually considered to be death, since it is not, perhaps they should be reconsidered.

Here's one reason for considering that death (not the afterlife, but actual death) is bad (even though it is nirvana-esque). Suppose that you were given the option of living the rest of your life or being dead in a join-the-universe-and-become-Dust sort of way. Would you choose to die if death were neutral (that is if death were an experiential blank)? Presumably nobody with a life that had positive value would trade it for something neutral. To do so would be irrational. But what about the second possibility—that becoming Dust was positive in nature? Here, I suppose that some would opt for that, but it is far from certain that most people would give up their positive experiences (along with their negative ones) for such a constant and unvarying existence.[2]

While we can conclude that life may be preferable to death (for most or all depending on the details of what death is like), we haven't been given reason to think that death is bad. In our world death is bad because of what it deprives us of or because of the desires it frustrates, but what we are deprived of or what desires are actually frustrated depends greatly on our circumstances. Let's consider each in turn.

Suppose that I have been offered a teaching position at Jordan College, which I must accept prior to December 1st of this year or the offer will expire. Suppose further that I do nothing with respect to the offer (it simply expires) and on January 15th of the following year I am devoured by an armored bear. While it may be plausible to suppose that my death deprived me of certain things, it is not plausible to suppose that my death deprived me of the job at Jordan College. That offer was already off the table. Similarly, the good things in life are already off the table at the point in which the residents of the world of the dead choose death. The only things that death deprives them of are boredom and pain. The good things that life has to offer are well in the past. So the Deprivation View cannot account for the badness of death, since death doesn't actually deprive anyone of anything good (nor will it, as the afterlife is, by hypothesis, unchanging in its essential features).

The Desire Frustration View doesn't fare much better. Suppose that I desire to be a professional baseball player someday. This desire may be strong, but given that it is not ever going to be satisfied (I can't hit a curve ball, my vision is beginning to falter, and I am well into middle age), it is not plausible to suppose that death is bad because it frustrates this desire. Death will only be bad to the extent that it frustrates desires that have a reasonable chance of being fulfilled. Again, once one finds oneself in the world of the dead, there are very few desires (if any) beyond the desire for death that may ever come to fruition. So the badness of death cannot be accounted for by the Desire Frustration View, either.

---

[2] Admittedly I'm basing this claim on purely anecdotal evidence, but years of getting people's reactions to Nozick's "experience machine" thought experiment has taught me that people are seldom willing to trade their lives for another mode of existence no matter what one (hypothetically) offers them.

So where does this leave us? In the worlds of *His Dark Materials*. Death simply isn't a bad thing. Perhaps it's not as good as living, but it sure beats the afterlife. That's why the dead choose it!

The Magisterium

RANDALL AUXIER lives in a forgotten corner of New Denmark called Carbondale, where he teaches experimental theology to young witches from the Shawnee Forest Clan. In return for esoteric instruction, they pretend to be ordinary undergraduates at Southern Illinois University. This past year he led them on a field trip to the Tori degli Angeles, and lost only a few to the specters. In spite of his years, his dæmon hasn't settled yet, although her favored sleeping form is as a gigantic housecat.

PAUL BAER is an assistant professor in the School of Public Policy at Georgia Tech in Atlanta, and a hell of a (part-time) philosopher. He holds an interdisciplinary Ph.D. from the Energy and Resources Group at UC Berkeley, and is often confused about his academic identity. His work focuses on climate change, and he has written extensively on ethical issues related to climate policy; he is also co-founder of the environmental group EcoEquity. He's married to Angie Harris, a full-time philosopher, who tries to keep him philosophically honest.

ABROL FAIRWEATHER loves teaching Philosophy so much that he splits time between the University of San Francisco, San Francisco State University, and Las Positas College. He received his Ph.D. in Philosophy from UC Santa Barbara, has published in the area of Virtue Epistemology, and is pursuing a recent interest in Philosophy of Emotion. His personal interests are focused on his wonderful daughter Barbara, ridiculously hot Bikram yoga classes, and an occasional leap into the cool Abyss.

HANNAH FINLEY is a Ph.D. student at UMass Amherst, where she studies anything philosophical that crosses her path as long as it does not look hard. She is particularly interested in the ethics of rights and the metaphysics of personal identity, and wonders if her dæmon violates her rights by failing to reveal himself as a part of her personal identity. However, she suspects that he is a squirrel.

RICHARD GREENE is Associate Professor of Philosophy at Weber State University. He received his Ph.D. in Philosophy from the University of California, Santa Barbara. He has published papers in epistemology, metaphysics, and ethics. Richard's dæmon hasn't settled yet, but it currently takes the following forms: a zombie movie, a video game, a nap, and a pastrami sandwich.

ANGELA RHYAN HARRIS is a Ph.D. candidate at the University of Utah and has had the privilege of being a visiting scholar at Rutgers University for the past two years. She wrote her Master's thesis on Nietzsche's ethics. Her philosophical appetites are insatiable. She has research interests in nearly every area of philosophy. She is completing her dissertation on the metaphysics of personal identity, practical identity, moral philosophy, and philosophy of psychology. Angela has spent a lot of time thinking about possible worlds and frequently wonders which of the possible worlds she's on. She is owned by five cats and two ferrets who closely supervise and assist her when she writes. She suspects any one or all of them are her dæmons, but she hasn't figured out how to see dæmons yet.

MARGARET MACKEY is a professor in the School of Library and Information Studies at the University of Alberta. There she shares an office with Lyra and many other toys, all of whom have ontological complexes about their literary and artifactual identity. She has written many books and articles on the subject of literacy in print and other media. Her most recent book is *Mapping Recreational Literacies: Contemporary Adults at Play* (2007).

NICOLAS MICHAUD teaches philosophy at the University of North Florida, Jacksonville University, The Art Institute of Jacksonville, and Florida Community College at Jacksonville. He is very hairy. Due to that and his love of the cold he believes that he is actually an armored polar bear. He is still disappointed that no one seems to understand his desire to eat the hearts of his enemies.

RACHEL ROBISON is pursuing a Ph.D. in Philosophy at UMass, Amherst. She loves both pop culture and philosophy (the former slightly more than the latter). Her work has appeared in *Quentin Tarantino and*

Philosophy and *The Legend of Zelda and Philosophy*. Like Lyra, Rachel has had a lot of problems with Authority.

MARY HARRIS RUSSELL is Professor Emerita of English at Indiana University Northwest. Previously, the closest that she'd come to philosophy was at Berkeley, studying works of spiritual advice for women hermits. Preferring not to live a hermit's life, she later headed in the direction of children's literature as well as reviewing children's books for the *Chicago Tribune*. Most recently, she has been writing about both Philip Pullman and Aidan Chambers, as well as developing the obscure hobby of collecting folding writing desks, a.k.a. slopes.

KIERA VACLAVIK is Lecturer in French and Comparative Literature at Queen Mary, University of London. She has published a range of articles about children's literature, especially that involving forms of subterranean travel. Her nearest equivalent in the *His Dark Materials* trilogy is probably Dame Hannah, although she hasn't yet given up aspirations to Mary Malone's adventurousness or Mrs. Coulter's glamour.

WAYNE YUEN teaches at Ohlone College in Fremont, California and has published essays in *The Undead and Philosophy* and *Terminator and Philosophy*. He is co-editing the forthcoming *Neil Gaiman and Philosophy*. He has an actual alethiometer in the shape of an oversized black billiard ball, but it keeps telling him to ask again later.

The Index of
Forbidden Thoughts